"This is a clear and thoughtful judicial study of the event that lies at the heart of the Christian faith. It should appeal to a wide readership. It both poses a fair challenge to the interested enquirer and also provides real encouragement to the believer that there is a solidly rational basis to the faith in which we live and which we seek to commend to others."

Mark Hedley, Hon. Professor of Law at Liverpool Hope University and former High Court Judge

"What a great idea to have a lawyer look at the evidence for Jesus' resurrection, much as he would if presiding at a trial! Thoroughly researched, easy to read but not lightweight, with summaries at each chapter's end, this book will arm believer and doubter alike with the evidence necessary to make a decision about a potentially life-changing story."

Revd Rob White

"In these days we are familiar with the comment that science is based on evidence whereas religion is based on blind faith and not on evidence. The fundamental tenets of the Christian faith include the statement that Jesus Christ rose from the dead. This is a statement that a particularly basic assertion is true.

"Graeme Smith has had a considerable career as a District Judge and in this well-written book he has approached the evidence for this assertion as a judge would do, inviting the reader to follow him. He requires that the reader should approach the question with an open mind. He marshals the evidence in an even-handed way, with no technicalities and without excessive detail. He then sums up and invites the reader to reach his or her own conclusion.

"I found his approach very refreshing. It is obvious that he writes with a wide knowledge of the relevant literature but the reader is not burdened with this except in so far as is necessary for an appreciation of the central issue. While science develops by the formulation of hypotheses to explain and connect observations, and further evidence may require the hypotheses to be modified, this is not true so far as this tenet of Christianity is concerned. Hence the importance of this book."

The Rt Hon. the Lord Mackay of Clashfern, former Lord Chancellor

Was the Tomb Empty?

A lawyer weighs the evidence
for the resurrection

GRAEME SMITH

MONARCH
BOOKS

Oxford, UK & Grand Rapids, Michigan, USA

Published by Monarch Books
an imprint of
Lion Hudson plc
Wilkinson House, Jordan Hill Road,
Oxford OX2 8DR, England
Email: monarch@lionhudson.com
www.lionhudson.com/monarch

ISBN 978 0 85721 528 4
e-ISBN 978 0 85721 529 1

First edition 2014

Acknowledgements
Biblical quotations are from the Holy Bible: New International Version, anglicised edition, copyright © 1973, 1978, 1984, 2011 by Biblica Inc. Used by permission of Hodder & Stoughton, a member of the Hodder Headline Group. All rights reserved.
p. 12: Extract from "Why I am not a Christian" by Ralph Jones in *Christianity* magazine copyright © Ralph Jones, February 2013. Used by permission of Ralph Jones and *Christianity* magazine.
pp. 133–34: Extracts from *Roman Society and Roman Law in the New Testament* by Sherwin White copyright © Sherwin White, 1963. Used by permission of Oxford University Press.
p. 136: Extract from *Fern-seed and Elephants* by C.S. Lewis copyright © C.S. Lewis Pte. Ltd. 1975. Extract reprinted by permission of The C.S. Lewis Company.

A catalogue record for this book is available from the British Library

Printed and bound in the UK, January 2014, LH26

Contents

Appendices

Acknowledgements

The idea of this book has been in my mind for many years, but without the help and support of several people it would have stayed there! Above all, I am very grateful to my long-suffering family and in particular my wife Helen, for her encouragement at each step of the process as she has put up with the whole process of getting the ideas out of my head and into a finished product.

Additionally, I am very grateful to Robin Croxon, who first encouraged me to sit down and begin writing; to Richard Herkes, who has enabled me to produce a complete, coherent text; to Gordon Tubbs, Alan Charlesworth, and Roy Pitcher, who have read and commented on the draft text; and to Tony Collins and his colleagues at Monarch who have made the publishing process so easy for me.

Although several people have commented on the text, I of course remain fully responsible for any errors which have survived this scrutiny.

Verdict!

The room falls silent as the door opens. Every eye focuses on the procession that enters. First comes a solemn figure robed in black; then twelve people – men, women, old, young, black, and white, from every walk of life. All are anonymous to the watchers, chosen at random. For days they have sat silently, watching and listening. For hours they have deliberated in secret, forbidden from ever revealing the content of their discussions. But now for a few moments they have become the sole focus of attention and their simple answer to a single question will determine the future of one person.

They move purposefully to their seats as those watching try to discern the slightest hint of the decision from their faces, their body language, whether they make or avoid eye contact. Once they are seated, another black-robed figure stands and begins reading words that have been read out every day for generations in courts across the land:

"Members of the jury, have you reached a verdict on which you are all agreed?"

"Yes."

"Do you find the defendant guilty, or not guilty?"

The delivery of the verdict by a jury is without doubt one of the most dramatic scenes in our legal system. There may be other tense moments as advocates try to undermine the evidence of witnesses, although these are rarely as exciting as portrayed in TV courtroom dramas! But the tension surrounding the delivery of the verdict is unequalled. Following days of evidence and legal submission, the judge, witnesses, advocates, members of the public and sometimes the press, and most importantly the defendant and the victim, will have been waiting for hours or even days with absolutely no indication of what is happening in the jury room. Suddenly a message is received that the jury is ready. Everyone returns to the courtroom to await their arrival; the defendant returns to discover his or her fate.

Dramatic though the delivery of a verdict is, it is in fact the conclusion of a painstaking and detailed consideration of the evidence. This is usually completely lacking from films and TV dramas, which tend to imply that court cases are dealt with in minutes rather than hours or days. In the real world, however, precisely because the decision of the jury can have such dramatic implications for the future of the defendant, it is essential that the evidence be considered and challenged thoroughly.

This book is just such a consideration of the evidence concerning Jesus' resurrection, and so it is deliberately painstaking and detailed. However, I hope that at its conclusion readers will feel something of the drama of a jury verdict as they reach their own conclusions.

And remember that, however complex a trial may be, its jury is always made up of twelve ordinary people – they could include me or you. Our legal system depends on the ability and commitment of such people, and only very rarely does a jury let down the system. The trial process essentially helps the jury to make the right decision. This book is intended to help readers to make the right decision, and there is no reason why any reader of this book cannot consider carefully the evidence and arrive at a fair, and safe, verdict.

How to Handle the Evidence

Recently I was struck by two very different articles in a magazine. One was by Christian writer and speaker Jeff Lucas and the other by self-described "militant atheist" Ralph Jones. The first examined the doubts that assail believers from time to time and concluded, "Doubt is just part of the normal Christian journey – an unwelcome companion, perhaps, but one that we need not fear."[1] The second explained the reasons why he found the Christian faith unreasonable and unbelievable.

Two kinds of doubt

This book is written for people who can identify with either of these positions – the doubts of a believer or the scepticism of one who does not believe.

I am a judge by profession, so it is perhaps not surprising that I wish to examine the evidence for Christian faith – and especially its pivotal event, the resurrection of Jesus of Nazareth from the dead – from a legal perspective. I was particularly challenged to do this when I read about a case brought in Italy by Luigi Cascioli against his local parish priest Enrico Righi for "abusing popular credulity" by teaching the historical existence of Jesus. Father Righi was ordered to appear in court to prove that Jesus did exist. (See, for example, Richard Owen's article posted on *The Times* online on 3 January 2006, which perversely appears in the European football section.)

Presumably he succeeded in making his case, as Mr Cascioli's claim was dismissed!

So I decided to attempt an analysis of the evidence as a court would do.

Christians are often portrayed as dogmatic, fully convinced that their views are right. Yet in my experience most Christians wrestle with doubts. Although some well-publicized figures make free and easy pronouncements at times, the vast majority of Christians are more circumspect. So while some may interpret the latest tragic disaster – say, an earthquake – as a judgment from God, most would be asking themselves questions. How does God's sovereignty interact with human free will? And if a natural disaster really were an "act of God" as the insurance companies like to tell us, how might this be consistent with God's love?

And doubt is not the only assailant facing a believer today. As "Western" society moves away from its Judeo-Christian foundations, it is no longer socially beneficial to profess Christian faith. In fact it can be positively disadvantageous to do so. Although talk of persecution would be a huge exaggeration at the present time, Christians do face criticism and ridicule for holding onto their faith in the modern world.

So why do so many people cling to belief? There may be several reasons, but my own experience is that the Christian faith provides the only satisfying explanation of a number of puzzles. These include questions about the origin and nature of the universe, moral challenges, and the riddle of Jesus' resurrection.

Why is there something rather than nothing? Who or what created the universe? Why is the universe so ideally suited to the emergence of life?

Why do people across the world have a sense of right and wrong, even though the content of moral codes may vary between societies? Why do people have a propensity to believe in something beyond this world?

And what are we to make of the staggering claim – ridiculous to some – that Jesus rose from the dead?

I am not a cosmologist, physicist, philosopher, or anthropologist, and so it is not for me to present a detailed response to the first two groups of questions. In any event, although I believe that answers to those questions indicate the existence of a divine being, even a personal one, they do not point unequivocally to the God portrayed by Christians. However, having spent twenty-seven years dealing with the assembling, presenting, and evaluating of evidence, I do feel qualified to analyse the historical data surrounding Jesus' resurrection.

I referred earlier to atheist Ralph Jones's explanation why he could not believe the Christian faith. He asserted that "there is not, first and foremost, a shred of truth in any of the extraordinary claims it makes. There is no way one can go from reading about a high-profile Bronze Age preacher in Israel to believing that he was born of a virgin, that he was resurrected, and that he is therefore the Son of God." He elaborated:

> The argument seems to me rather circular: why do
> Christians believe Jesus rose from the dead? Because
> he is the Son of God. Why do Christians believe Jesus
> is the Son of God? Because he rose from the dead. To
> believe Jesus was resurrected on the basis of historical
> evidence would require a staggering level of credulity,
> and I don't know how many Christians would argue
> that the case could be made. Why, therefore, does there
> exist this desperate urge to draw gargantuan claims
> from pitiful evidence? Why not concede to a very
> obvious defeat? It is this wishful thinking, this need to
> have comforting and childish explanations that defy
> logic, that informs my rejection of religion.[2]

To meet this objection I can say emphatically that my belief that Jesus is the Son of God plays no part at all in my conclusion (from the evidence) that he rose from the dead. On the other hand, my conclusion that he rose from the dead is a fundamental foundation of my belief that he is the Son of God.

When Christians argue sloppily

In fact I sympathize with much of what Ralph Jones says about the way many Christians try to justify their belief in Jesus' resurrection. Circular arguments will not do. Nor will an approach that urges us simply to "have faith" and not to question what the Bible says.

Historically speaking, many books on the resurrection have taken the reliability of the four Gospels as read – they have "taken them as gospel" as the saying goes – and their arguments both start and end with these accounts. Such an approach may have been acceptable to previous generations, but the historical reliability of the Gospels is no longer something we can take for granted. A number of serious issues arise when we rely on the Gospels by themselves as proof of the resurrection. Of course they are vital evidence, but they are not the only evidence.

There is another approach adopted by some Christians, and that is to rely on quotations from eminent Christian lawyers. The one used most frequently is that attributed to Lord Chief Justice Darling:

> in its favour as a living truth there exists such
> overwhelming evidence, positive and negative, factual
> and circumstantial, that no intelligent jury in the world
> could fail to bring in a verdict that the resurrection
> story is true.

While the quotation is superficially impressive, it suffers from two overwhelming objections: (1) Lord Darling was never Lord Chief Justice and (2) there seems to be no actual record of Lord Darling (who was a judge) ever saying this! Even worse, I have seen examples of the same quotation being attributed to other lawyers, most notably Lord Denning. Although Lord Denning was a Christian, it is clear that he never used these words, which seem to have been put in his mouth by a process similar to Chinese whispers. In an age where information is immediately available at the click of a mouse, problems like this can quickly be exposed, and then they inevitably undermine the whole argument in favour of the resurrection. Is it any wonder that people like Ralph Jones describe the evidence as pitiful?

This is not to say that quotations cannot be useful if used appropriately. In my view, we should apply rules that are similar to those used by the courts when previous case law ("precedent") is relied upon. Comments by judges need to be properly sourced, authoritative and read in context.

A good example of the need to read in context is the use of the phrase, used in several motor accident cases, that a car is potentially a "lethal weapon" (for example Goundry -v- Hepworth [2005] EWCA Civ 1738 – see the end of this chapter for an explanation of this kind of reference). These words are relied upon regularly by lawyers acting for pedestrians injured by motorists, to support their claim that the motorist is at fault. I have seen a barrister try to rely on these words without reading on to what followed. If he had, it would have been clear that, if a pedestrian stepped into the path of a car without any warning, in circumstances where the driver was driving with reasonable care, the driver would not be at fault. Since that was precisely what was alleged to have happened in the case which his client was pursuing, the quotation in fact assisted the defendant motorist!

In view of all this, I have endeavoured to abide by certain principles throughout this book: to trace appropriate quotations to their source, check that they are authoritative, and respect their original context.

Sceptics do it too

Having made these criticisms of some of the "evidence" offered by some Christians, I feel the same can be said about those who seek to disprove the resurrection. Quite simply, some critics do not seem to realize they are adopting double standards. In their eagerness to find evidence which will disprove the resurrection, they are quick to accept theories which have little if any reliable evidential basis. We will see examples of this approach in Chapters 1, 10, and 17.

Here is an example. In 2012 a small scrap of papyrus was discovered. Written in ancient Egyptian Coptic script in the fourth century, it was believed to be a copy of a "gospel" originally written in Greek late in the second century. Controversially, it included a reference by Jesus to "my wife". While serious academics were guarded in their response (and indeed some considered it not to be an authentic document), others rushed to confirm that it established Jesus' married status. But this would be like the discovery of a single document written 150 years after the death of Cliff Richard, saying that he had been married (at the time of writing he is not). Not only would this not be good evidence, it would not be evidence at all, as it refers to no source and it would be produced long after Cliff's contemporaries had died.

So if you do not believe that Jesus rose from the dead, or if you struggle with doubts, I invite you to consider the evidence with an open mind. In this book the evidence will be presented in a way that avoids both circular reasoning and the need for startling levels of credulity.

References

References to the Bible text are given in the conventional format of the name of the book followed by the chapter and verse numbers separated by a colon. Thus John 20:25–29 refers to verses 25 to 29 of chapter 20 of the Gospel of John.

Judgments in cases are generally reported in this format: [2005] EWCA Civ 1738. The date in square brackets is the date of the report. The letters identify the source of the report (e.g. EWCA means England & Wales Court of Appeal; WLR means Weekly Law Reports). The concluding number is the page number in the report. For anyone who wishes to do what I have recommended, and go back to the source, the best starting point is the website www.bailii.org (the British and Irish Legal Information Institute), which provides free access to a wide range of case reports.

Notes have been kept to a reasonable minimum, and these appear at the end of the book. Books are sourced in the main text for quick and easy reference by citing the author and date of publication – full details appear in the Bibliography. I am grateful to all those copyright holders who have granted permission for me to reproduce extracts.

PART 1
OPENING SUBMISSIONS

CHAPTER ONE

Jesus

Who?

In a London school a teenager with no church connections hears the Christmas story for the first time. His teacher tells it well and he is fascinated by this amazing story. Risking his friends' mockery, after the lesson he thanks her for the story. One thing had disturbed him, so he asks: "Why did they give the baby a swear word for his name?"

Stuart Murray (2004)

For many people today, the only time they hear or use the names "Jesus" or "Christ" is as swear words. This is surprising, given the extent to which the story of Jesus has influenced society. Our two main public holidays originated as celebrations of Jesus' birth (Christmas) and his death and resurrection (Easter), although they are probably now better known for Father Christmas and chocolate eggs. History itself is reckoned in our society by reference to the year when Jesus is supposed to have been born, so we have BC (before Christ) and AD (Anno Domini – in the year of the Lord).

More subtly than this, our language is full of expressions taken from the life and teaching of Jesus: a "good Samaritan" is someone who goes out of his way to help a stranger; FT5K is a sandwich shop named from an abbreviation of "feed the five thousand"; "Judas" is a term used for someone who betrays; "carrying my cross" is a description of having to bear some great trouble or burden; "walking on water" describes someone who has been remarkably successful; and so on. It is unlikely that most people know the origins of such phrases, but they show the extent to which the story of Jesus is ingrained in our society.

A spectrum

A large proportion of society may know little or nothing about Jesus, but even among those who do recognize the historical Jesus there is a huge spectrum of views. At one end is the orthodox Christian view, set out centuries ago in the Nicene creed. Here is the section on Jesus:

> We believe in one Lord, Jesus Christ,
> the only Son of God,
> eternally begotten of the Father,
> God from God, Light from Light,
> true God from true God,
> begotten, not made,
> of one Being with the Father.
> Through him all things were made.
> For us and for our salvation
> he came down from heaven:
> by the power of the Holy Spirit
> he became incarnate from the Virgin Mary,
> and was made man.
> For our sake he was crucified under Pontius Pilate;
> he suffered death and was buried.
> On the third day he rose again
> in accordance with the Scriptures;
> he ascended into heaven
> and is seated at the right hand of the Father.

He will come again in glory to judge the living
   and the dead,
and his kingdom will have no end.[3]

Although an ancient formula, it is still repeated regularly by Christians throughout the world, and it contains statements of belief which are both theological and historical.

At the other end of the spectrum is the view that the story of Jesus is nothing more than a work of fiction – albeit perhaps a very profound and influential work of fiction. According to this view, Jesus was no more a historical figure than Hercules or Mary Poppins.

Between these two views of Jesus lies a vast array of others. Some people see him as a great teacher or holy man; some see him as a martyr; some see him as a prophet. The last of those views is that of Islam, which accepts Jesus as one of the great prophets, born of the Virgin Mary, and a performer of miracles. However, Islam emphatically denies that Jesus was in any way divine, or that he rose from the dead, or even that he was crucified and died.[4]

Everyone loves a conspiracy

Conspiracy theories abound in every area of life. Many people seem very receptive to claims that the "official" version of events is a conspiracy to conceal the truth, whether the subject is history (the sinking of the *Titanic*, the holocaust), death (Elvis, John F. Kennedy, Princess Diana), health (MMR), politics (9/11 and the ensuing "war against terror"), or the universe (UFOs and alien abduction).

The courts are not immune to this approach. Not infrequently a claim is brought by someone who is convinced they are the victim of a conspiracy. I remember well as a young articled clerk (the old term for a trainee solicitor) meeting a new client who claimed to have been knocked down by a Rolls Royce. Initially her claim sounded genuine, but as the interview proceeded she claimed that this was a weekly occurrence, engineered by Nazis! As I showed her out, she said in a loud voice across a crowded waiting room, "You'll be hearing from the Pope about this!" I'm still waiting.

This is an extreme example; many are much more sophisticated and believable, at least superficially. While occasionally such claims have some basis in fact, more usually they are based on no evidence at all, or on supposed evidence taken totally out of context. Indeed, the lack of evidence is sometimes relied on as proof of the conspiracy – the evidence does not exist because it has been destroyed by the conspirators, and lawyers and judges who reach negative conclusions are often simply added to the list of those conspirators.

Many people have a similar view of the traditional Christian story. The statement "Everyone loves a conspiracy" is made by two different characters in Dan Brown's book *The Da Vinci Code* (pages 232, 500). It seems that these words were prophetic, as the book became an international bestseller, telling of a conspiracy by the church to suppress the fact that Jesus was married to Mary Magdalene and that they had a child. This book was a popular restatement of ideas that have appeared before, for example in the bestselling *The Holy Blood and the Holy Grail*, which was described in a judgment by Mr Justice Peter Smith as being "at the far end of conjecture".[5] (For a closer look into the *Da Vinci Code* phenomenon see Appendix 1, and for comments on *The Holy Blood and the Holy Grail* see Appendix 3.)

Invariably such books challenge the "orthodox" story of Jesus, positioning it as less than faithful to what really happened. This is unparalleled in any other religion. (Although there are a few such books, for example in relation to the Jewish ark of the covenant, these pale into insignificance beside the sheer volume of books challenging the orthodox Christian story.) It seems that there are huge numbers of people receptive to the idea that the church has manipulated and concealed the true story of Jesus.

Know the truth

Jesus is recorded as saying that "the truth will set you free" (John 8:32). The purpose of this book is to look at the evidence to see if the truth about Jesus can be established. I believe that it can, but this is a question which you will need to answer for yourself. As to whether this truth can then lead on to freedom, that can only be established by experience. The answer of millions of Christians throughout history and across the world is a resounding "yes", but this will carry little if any weight with someone unconvinced that the basic story is true. However, it may provide a small but tantalizing incentive to embark upon the journey in the first place.

Rather than attempting to analyse evidence about the whole of Jesus' life, we will focus principally on that relating to his resurrection. This is because, in the words of the eminent lawyer Professor Sir Norman Anderson (1969, page 84):

> the belief that Christ rose from the dead is not an
> optional extra, superimposed on his life and death
> to give a happy ending to what might otherwise be
> regarded as a tragedy of infinite beauty overshadowed
> by doubts as to whether it was not, after all, a supreme
> example of magnificent defeat. On the contrary, it is the
> linchpin.

Put simply, the resurrection of Jesus is at the very heart of the Christian faith. As Paul said bluntly, "if Christ has not been raised, our preaching is useless and so is your faith" (1 Corinthians 15:14). If the evidence for the resurrection is lacking, then there is little point looking any further, except for selecting parts of Jesus' teaching which may help us in our daily living. However, if the evidence for the resurrection is compelling, this will throw a very different light on Jesus' life and teaching, and will lead us to much more profound questions. As one Christian writer puts it, "The resurrection of Jesus Christ is one of the *most wicked, vicious, heartless hoaxes ever foisted upon the minds of men*, or it is the most fantastic fact of history" (McDowell 1981, 1998, page 179). Let us weigh carefully the evidence to ascertain which it is.

Before we journey into the evidence, we need to establish some ground rules, and this is the purpose of the next few chapters. We shall start by considering the nature of history itself because if, as stated by the character Leigh Teabing in *The Da Vinci Code,* "history is always written by the winners … always a one-sided account" (Brown 2003, page 343), then we must ask whether there is any basis on which we could ever accept that the story of Jesus is historical?

SUMMARY

- There is a wide spectrum of views about Jesus.
- Many believe that the church has conspired to hide the truth about Jesus.
- We will focus on the central Christian claim about Jesus – that he rose from the dead.

CHAPTER 2

History

History became legend; legend became myth;
and for two and a half thousand years the ring passed
out of all knowledge.

These are among the opening words of the first film in *The Lord of the Rings* trilogy, explaining why no one had any memory of the ring of power. Today, many people seem to believe that Christians have operated in precisely the reverse direction, and that they have taken a myth or a legend and have elevated it to the status of history.

History, legend and myth

One dictionary defines a *myth* as "a traditional story which contains ideas or beliefs about ancient times or natural events, and which forms part of the beliefs of a group even though it is not founded on fact". A *legend* is defined as "a story (which may or may not be true) handed down from the past". We will look at the definition of *history* shortly, but will note at this stage that it is concerned with facts.

So, as we look at the story of Jesus, are we in the realm of history, or are we considering a myth or a legend?

C. S. Lewis is probably best known for his *Chronicles of Narnia*. However, as a former Professor of Mediaeval and Renaissance English at Cambridge University, he was well placed to comment on the literary quality of the story of Jesus.

In relation to the suggestion that the Gospel records are legends, he commented as follows (Lewis 2000, page 40):

> Now, as a literary historian, I am perfectly convinced that whatever else the Gospels are they are not legends. I have read a great deal of legend and I am quite clear that they are not the same sort of thing. They are not artistic enough to be legends. From an imaginative point of view they are clumsy, they don't work up to things properly. Most of the life of Jesus is totally unknown to us, as is the life of anyone else who lived at that time, and no people building up legend would allow that to be so. Apart from bits of the Platonic dialogues, there are no conversations that I know of in ancient literature like the Fourth Gospel. There is nothing, even in modern literature, until about 100 years ago when the realistic novel came into existence.

The style of the Gospel records, then, is not that of legend. In addition, consider the timescale involved in the story of Jesus. As we shall see, written references to the death and resurrection of Jesus came into existence by the early 50s AD at the latest. That was only some twenty years after the events in question. Unlike the case of the 2,500-year period in *The Lord of the Rings*, it is impossible to see how a myth or legend could be established in such a short period of time.

To demonstrate this, we can consider events in recent history. The death of President Kennedy in 1963 still attracts conspiracy theories, yet no one seriously doubts that he did die, or even that he was shot. And we don't need the film footage that exists to make the case – many people still remember vividly where they were and what they were doing when they first heard the news of his death.

This can be seen even more clearly with the death of

someone important to us. I remember the day I was told of the death of a close friend, more than thirty years ago, as if it were yesterday.

It therefore seems not just unlikely but impossible that a myth or a legend concerning Jesus, which diverged substantially from actual historical truth, could develop within such a short period of time. That is not to say that everything written in the Gospels must be true, but it does mean that we can and should approach the whole question of the story of Jesus as history.

What is history?

Students at school may think they know what history is, but in fact the nature of history is a matter of considerable debate among academics.

Professor G. R. Elton (1969, page 51) gave a straightforward definition of history: "The study of history, then, amounts to a search for the truth." However, E. H. Carr (1961, pages 24, 3) took issue with this, and provided a more complex definition, stressing the role of the historian:

> History … is a continuous process of interaction
> between the historian and his facts, an unending
> dialogue between the present and the past … History
> consists of a corpus of ascertainable facts. The facts are
> available to the historian in documents, inscriptions and
> so on, like fish on the fishmonger's slab. The historian
> collects them, takes them home and cooks and serves
> them in whatever style appeals to him.

More recently, there have been numerous definitions of history, most of which are more sophisticated. It is not the function of this work to discuss in detail the nature of history, nor to provide a decisive definition (if that were even possible). However, it is necessary to understand what is meant by the statement that "the story of Jesus is history".

One of the challenges facing us is that the word "history" is used to describe several different concepts, including:

1. The total content of time, including past, present and future (as in "the whole of human history").

2. The total content of the past only.

3. The content of the past in so far as it can be discovered from evidence.

4. The content of the past which has actually been discovered.

5. Records of past events written by historians.

6. A vague and generally agreed picture of the past.

7. The study of the past.

In addition, the word "historic" is used to indicate something significant in history.

Napoleon and Abba

No one disputes that events happened in the past (which we shall call "facts"), but there is substantial dispute about the extent to which we can know these facts. Napoleon famously said that "history is the version of past events that people have decided to agree upon".

In fact Napoleon himself provides us with an excellent case study of the nature of history. Perhaps one of the "best-known" statements about Napoleon is "At Waterloo Napoleon did surrender", which comes from the 1974 Eurovision Song

Contest winner by Abba. Unfortunately all Napoleonic scholars agree that this statement is false! Napoleon undoubtedly retreated from Waterloo, but he did not surrender. All historians of the period agree on a basic body of facts, including:

(a) There were a number of battles between 16 and 18 June 1815.

(b) In those battles French armies under the overall command of Napoleon fought against Prussian armies under the overall command of Blucher and mixed multi-national armies under the overall command of the Duke of Wellington.

(c) The final conflict took place on 18 June, just south of the village of Waterloo in Belgium.

(d) At the conclusion of the conflict the French forces retreated.

(e) A number of senior allied commanders were either killed (e.g. General Picton) or injured (e.g. the Earl of Uxbridge and the Prince of Orange).

There are also numerous facts which are not agreed, including the precise timing of individual elements within the conflict, the exact disposition of the units within the armies, and the numbers of casualties on each side.

Finally, there are significant disputes between historians as to issues such as the respective contributions of the English and Prussian armies, and the tactical merits (or lack of them) of decisions made by commanders including Marshall Ney and the Prince of Orange.

Notwithstanding the uncertainties in relation to the details, it could not seriously be suggested that we cannot know, with a very high probability of accuracy, the basic facts about the battle.

The story of Jesus

Whatever else is contentious, it cannot be disputed that the story of Jesus is historic. It resulted in the rapid spread of a set of beliefs which are now held by a proportion of the world's population larger than any other comparable set of beliefs. However, in what sense is the story *history*?

On the basis that it involves, to a greater or lesser extent, events that actually happened, it is "history" within meanings (1) and (2) above. It has been written about extensively, and so is clearly "history" within meaning (5). Most people, if asked, would probably accept the fact of Jesus' existence, and might have a general impression of his life, so it is also "history" within meaning (6). But meanings (3) and (4) – its relation to the discovery of evidence – are more problematic at two levels.

First, it is strongly disputed how much has actually been discovered about the story, and this will occupy a substantial part of later chapters. But the fact that there is no agreement about every detail of the story does not mean that the story itself is not history. If that was the test to be applied, then we would have no "history" at all. Indeed, "history" in meaning (7) involves the use of many skills to seek to arrive at "history" in meaning (3), by discovering and analysing the evidence available.

The second problem relates specifically to the story of Jesus, rather than to the study of history generally. According to orthodox Christian belief, the story of Jesus involves events which took place *in* history, but which also transcend or stand *outside* history. In his commentary *Matthew for Everyone* New Testament scholar Tom Wright comments that the writer of the Gospel of Matthew "clearly intended to write of something that had actually happened, something that not only changed the women's hearts but *had torn a hole in normal history*" (page 200, emphasis mine). It is possible to study the facts of Jesus' life and death, but how can we consider, as a matter of history, the claims that he was God incarnate and that he rose from the dead?

History is populated by people whose every word and action can be scrutinized, so long as they leave evidence behind them. In the same way, we can scrutinize what Jesus said and did, what he ate and drank, and how he died. But how can we even begin to consider whether he was God? How can we expect to find an answer to the question of whether he rose from the dead, when not even the Gospel accounts record anyone witnessing the actual event? (And should we even describe it as an event?) History, in any of its meanings, simply has no precedent for these issues.

All is not lost

What, then, do we do at this stage? Is there any point in trying to proceed further? There are two opposing views:

1. As these matters are "outside" or "beyond" history, there is no point in trying to analyse the historical position. We must simply accept what God tells us in the Bible by faith.

2. As these matters are incapable of historical "proof", we must reject them, and accordingly there is no point in trying to analyse the historical position.

In my opinion, both views are flawed. The first view, which is held by some Christians, has the merit of accepting that when we are considering the actions of God, we are looking beyond history, and faith is required to be an "assurance about what we do not see" (Hebrews 11:1). However, this can be seen as, at best, a cop-out from serious thought and study and, at worst, a smokescreen to be used to hide our doubts. Some might cynically suggest here that for many Christians faith is being "certain of what is not true"! The fact that some matters are "beyond" history does not, and should not, preclude us from considering history where it intersects with those matters.

The second view presupposes that, because matters cannot be historically proved, they should be rejected. We shall turn to the question of "proof" in the next chapter; however, even if some matters cannot be "proved" in the same way as other historical events, this does not mean that they should be rejected without further ado. To do so is to arrive at the conclusion without first considering the evidence. What is required is a consideration of the historical evidence to see what light it can shed on these matters.

SUMMARY

- The story of Jesus should be considered as history, not myth or legend.
- The claims about Jesus go beyond history, but this does not mean that we cannot analyse the historical evidence.

CHAPTER 3

Proof

The proof of the pudding is in the eating.

This is a well-known and generally accepted saying, but it does not apply universally. Of course we would all prefer to be able to eat the pudding before deciding on its quality, but while we are able to "prove" many things by the direct evidence of our own eyes and ears (or, come to that, our own taste buds), we accept "proof" of many more things on the basis of indirect evidence.

For example, we are likely to place great weight on the reviews of puddings which appear in newspapers or on television. More seriously, we generally accept as true much of what we read in the newspaper or hear on the radio, or what we are told by our friends and family. If we did not do so, we would get very little done; if I require visual proof that a train is due to leave Euston Station in London, bound for Glasgow, at 5 p.m. next Tuesday before I'll even buy a ticket, I may find that there are no tickets left when I try to purchase one, and even if there are I will certainly end up paying a higher price!

The need to rely on sources other than our own senses is particularly relevant in matters of history, where we simply do not have the opportunity to be present as the events unfold. It is also the situation in any trial; the judge and jury will not have been present at the events which are being considered. In the case of A Local Authority -v- S. and W. and T. in 2004 Mr Justice Hedley said this:

Truth is an absolute but elusive concept, and the law, in recognising that, deals with it in terms of what can be proved. The fact that something cannot be proved does not mean it did not happen but only that it cannot be proved to the requisite standard that it did. That is the price society has to pay for human fallibility in the quest for truth.

[2004] EWHC 1270 Fam

In order to decide whether facts can be proved, courts rely on evidence, and the law has developed rules detailing how the relevant facts can be proved. In particular, the law sets out rules as to the *burden of proof* and the *standard of proof*, and these will be very helpful as we consider how any historical fact can be proved.

Consider an example which occupies courts every day of the week: road traffic accidents. Two cars collide. Each driver blames the other. At the trial the judge will determine who is responsible for the accident by considering the evidence, having heard "submissions" from lawyers representing the drivers and their insurers. To do this the judge will apply the rules as to the burden and standard of proof.

The burden of proof

The general rule as to the burden of proof is very simple: the person who makes an allegation must prove it. So in our example, if driver 1 brings a claim against driver 2, alleging that driver 2 caused the accident because of his negligent driving, the burden of proof would be on driver 1 to prove this. If he fails to do so, the claim will fail. It would not be necessary for driver 2 to prove another cause of the accident: if the judge was simply unable to form a view as to which driver was at fault, the claim would fail because the burden of proof had not been discharged by driver 1. Driver 2 may, of course, choose to suggest other possible causes of the accident, but the goal is to show that driver 1 has failed to satisfy the court that driver 2 was at fault.

The standard of proof

The standard of proof is more complex, because it varies in different types of case. Broadly speaking, there are two main tests which are used in English law (the same, or similar tests apply in numerous other nations, including Australia, Canada, and the USA). The first, used in most criminal cases, is "beyond reasonable doubt"; the second, used in most civil cases, is "on the balance of probabilities". The first requires the court to be "certain, so that it is sure", and the second requires the court to determine that something is "more likely than not".

In our example, driver 2 may end up facing a civil claim from driver 1, based on his negligent driving, and a criminal prosecution, for driving without due care and attention. Because of the different standards of proof which would apply to the two cases, he could lose the civil claim but be acquitted on the criminal prosecution, even if identical evidence was given at both trials.

Even within the civil standard of proof, the law will in practice require a greater certainty in respect of some facts. In a leading case Lord Nicholls said:

> The inherent probability or improbability of an event
> is itself a matter to take into account when weighing
> the probabilities and deciding whether, on balance, the
> event occurred. The more improbable the event, the
> stronger must be the evidence that it did occur before,
> in the balance of probabilities, its occurrence will be
> established.

Re: H. (Minors)(Sexual abuse: Standard of proof) [1996] AC 563

The House of Lords made it clear in a subsequent case (Re: B. (Children)[2008] UKHL 35) that the standard of proof remains the same – the balance of probabilities; however, the more improbable an event, the stronger the evidence which will be required to meet that standard. For example, a pupil alleging abduction by aliens as his reason for arriving late at school is likely to require much stronger evidence to satisfy his teacher than a pupil who alleges that his bus was cancelled.

The resurrection of Jesus

How, then, do the rules as to burden and standard of proof apply as we embark upon our task of considering the claims about Jesus? As we have seen, the traditional Christian teaching is that Jesus was divine and that he rose from the dead. Where does the burden of proof lie in relation to these claims, and what standard of proof applies?

Although there is no shortage of people claiming to be God, or to be the reincarnation of a character from history, we must start from the undoubted facts that generally people are not divine and do not rise from the dead. Therefore the burden of proof must be on those who seek to assert that Jesus was an exception to these basic facts. Further, the suggestion that Jesus was divine, and that he rose from the dead, is a serious assertion. Indeed, it is difficult to conceive of a more serious one. Even if the civil standard of proof applies, the facts demand the most cogent proof.

Some would go further, and would dispute that it is possible even to attempt to consider the claims, on the basis that God does not exist and therefore Jesus cannot have been divine and cannot have risen from the dead; in other words, the starting point must be that the Christian claims are self-evidently false. The events in question are not simply improbable, they are impossible. If a witness at a trial claimed to have been simultaneously in two different places, there would be no need to subject his evidence to any analysis, as it would be self-evidently false.

Here Christians naturally respond that there is no proof that God does not exist; to the contrary, there is good evidence that God does exist (including the evidence of Jesus' resurrection).

The best starting point, which would probably be accepted by most people, is to assume that there is no conclusive evidence one way or the other. Indeed, in reality that seems to be the position taken by even the most ardent atheist, Richard Dawkins. In his book *The God Delusion* he effectively reaches this conclusion in a closely reasoned chapter entitled "Why there almost certainly is no God".[6] Having considered six "finely tuned" fundamental constants required for the universe to allow life to evolve, he states (in Chapter 4) that a God capable of producing those constants would have to be "at least as improbable" as the combination of constants.

Of course, the fact that he has written and we can read his book means that the required combination of constants, however improbable, has occurred, and there is no logical reason why the same analysis cannot apply to the existence of God.

Ray's hips

A solicitor once dictated "Particulars of Claim" to his secretary, setting out the details of his client's claim arising from an accident. When he received the typed document back, he was very surprised to read in the middle of the document that "Ray's hips are locked together". He was surprised for a number of reasons: this was not what he had dictated; his client was not called Ray; the condition described would be physically impossible! What he had dictated was *res ipsa loquitor*, a Latin phrase still used by many lawyers despite attempts to eradicate Latin from civil claims. The phrase literally means "the thing speaks for itself " – in other words, something is self-evident. For example, if a moving vehicle collides with a parked car, it is not necessary to give full details of the negligence of the driver. It is sufficient to say *res ipsa loquitor*, because the cause of the collision is self-evident.

The limits of this concept are obvious. In the example just given, the driver might respond by saying that his vehicle had first been hit by another vehicle, and that is what caused the collision, so it was the fault of the third vehicle's driver. Or that he had reasonably swerved to avoid a pedestrian who had run out into the road, so it was the fault of the pedestrian. Alleging *res ipsa loquitor* does not finally determine a claim, but it throws the burden on the other party.

Some Christians would say *res ipsa loquitor* in relation to the resurrection. They would contend that the only possible explanation for the growth of the vibrant church based on the resurrection of Jesus, from a group of disparate individuals whose leader had just been brutally executed, is that Jesus was indeed raised from the dead.

On the face of it, there is considerable merit in this view. Many religions and other movements have survived the death of a charismatic leader, and have gone on to prosper. However, in those cases its adherents have not lived (and in many cases died) insisting that their leader was raised from the dead. Having said this, given the improbable nature of someone rising from the dead, and given the other explanations that have been suggested for the growth of the church (including the first disciples simply being mistaken), non-Christians are very unlikely to accept that the facts are self-evident. Accordingly, it is necessary to proceed and examine the evidence in some considerable detail, although we will return to this point when considering the evidence of the early church.

SUMMARY

- In considering the resurrection of Jesus, we are asking whether it can be proved.
- The onus is on those asserting the resurrection to prove that it did occur.
- Very cogent evidence will be required.

CHAPTER 4

Evidence

Thomas ... said to them, "Unless I see the nail marks
in his hands and put my finger where the nails were,
and put my hand into his side, I will not believe ...
Jesus told him, "Because you have seen me, you have
believed; blessed are those who have not seen and yet
have believed."

John 20:24–25, 29

A leading textbook (*Phipson on Evidence*, 2012, para 1–10)
states that the word "evidence" in judicial proceedings has
several meanings but is used in two main senses:

> Evidence, in the first sense, means the testimony,
> whether oral, documentary or real, which may be
> legally received in order to prove or disprove some fact
> in dispute. In the second sense it means the content of
> the testimony.

In subsequent chapters, we will consider the content of the
testimony we have about Jesus' resurrection. In this chapter,
we will give some preliminary consideration to the *form* of that
testimony: exactly what evidence is available, and how reliable
is it?

Acts of Parliament, Court Rules and decisions of the
courts lay down detailed and complex rules as to the nature
of reliable evidence and the conditions that must be satisfied

if the evidence is to be relied upon. These rules develop, of necessity, as the nature of the available evidence changes. A recent example is that of electronic documents and data and storage media, none of which were available only a generation ago. Court procedures are being adapted to deal with emails, databases, portable storage devices, metadata, and a whole host of other sources of evidence.

It is not necessary to examine the rules of evidence in detail (so you may breathe a sigh of relief, given that the current edition of *Phipson* runs to 1,496 pages). However, it is important to consider in general terms the types of evidence that are available when a trial is taking place. Generally, evidence falls into the following categories:

- Documents. (The "essence of a document is that it is something containing recorded information of some sort".[7])

- Witnesses. ("Direct evidence means that the existence of ... a fact is proved ... by the testimony or admissible declaration of someone who has himself perceived it".[8])

- Experts. (An expert provides "objective unbiased opinion in relation to matters within his expertise".[9])

- Real evidence. ("Material objects other than documents, produced for the inspection of the court, are commonly called real evidence. This, when available, is probably the most satisfactory kind of all."[10])

- Indirect or circumstantial evidence. ("Indirect or presumptive evidence means that other facts are thus proved, from which the existence of a given fact may be logically inferred."[11])

Before we consider the evidence for the resurrection of Jesus, we first need to consider what evidence we would and would not expect to find. As we are dealing with events which took place nearly 2,000 years ago, our only witnesses are those who have given us the records of the events. So we need to consider the nature of the records, and the extent to which they have been compiled by witnesses.

The New Testament documents

We live in an age of readily available mass media. Anything of note which happens will usually be almost instantly available on the internet, radio and television, and in newspapers soon afterwards. As well as formal sources of information such as news broadcasts, information will be readily available in blogs and on social networking sites. With such a huge amount of information it can be problematic deciding which is actually true.

When dealing with events that took place 2,000 years ago, we face a totally different problem. There is likely to be little information available, and we need to ask how much has survived and how accurate it is, particularly given the passage of time. When considering Jesus and his resurrection, it is instructive to compare the information available in relation to other people and events at around the same time in history. The *volume* of information is not, of itself, a guarantee of accuracy, but if there are *multiple sources* then this will enable us to be much more certain that the transmission of the information has not been corrupted. If there is only one copy of a document, then we can have no idea whether it is a true copy of the original. If we have two copies, then we can be a little more certain, unless there are differences between the two, in which case we may still have little idea which (if either) of the two is the better copy. However, as the number of early copies increases, we are much better able to compare them and to determine what the original is likely to have said.

Bearing this in mind, let us compare the copies of the New Testament documents which are available with copies of the following:

- Thucydides' *History of the Peloponnesian War* between Sparta and Athens in the fifth century BC. Thucydides was a Greek historian.

- Caesar's *Gallic War*. Julius Caesar wrote Commentarii de Bello Gallico, an account of nine years of warfare in Gaul, in the first century BC.

- Tacitus' *Histories*. Tacitus was a Roman senator and historian. These cover the period AD 69–96.

- Josephus' *Jewish War*. Josephus was a Jewish aristocrat who wrote a history of the war of AD 66–70 between the Romans and the Jews. He wrote as a witness of the events.

- The New Testament books.

We will compare the following features:

1. The believed date of production of the original document.

2. The oldest surviving copy.

3. The number of ancient copies available.

The comparison is most striking when shown as a table:[12]

Document	Thucydides	Caesar	Tacitus	Josephus	Gospels
1. Date of original	460–400 BC	58–50 BC	AD 100	AD 70	AD 65–90
2. Date of oldest surviving copy	AD 900 (plus a few first-century fragments)	AD 850	AD 800	5th Century (Latin translation); 10th century (Greek copy)	AD 350 (plus numerous fragments, the earliest dating AD 130 or earlier)
3. Time between 1 and 2	1,300 years (400 years from fragments)	900 years	700 years	400 years (from Latin translation); 900 years.	260 years (40 years from first fragment)
4. Number of copies	8	10	2	9	5,735[13]

It is worth pausing here to reflect on the magnitude of the difference between the source material available in respect of the New Testament and the other works we are considering – Metzger and Ehrman (1964, 2005, page 51) comment that the textual critic of the New Testament is "embarrassed by the wealth of the material". Not only are there many, many more copies available, but the earliest copies are much closer in time to the originals. Historians do not doubt the basic integrity of the works of Thucydides, Caesar, Tacitus or Josephus, so why should any different test be applied to the New Testament documents?

Indeed, the position is even more stark than the above table suggests. Although the earliest complete copies of the New Testament date back to AD 350, there are many earlier incomplete copies. The oldest yet identified is a tiny fragment of John's Gospel which is held in the John Rylands Library in Manchester, and is dated at AD 130 or earlier – only about forty years after the original is thought to have been written. Later fragments include much more material, including two thirds of John's Gospel in the Bodmer papyrus dated at around AD 200.

The evidence of witnesses

Of course, an abundance of documents does not necessarily mean that they are reliable. The fact that the *Harry Potter* books have sold millions of copies does not make the contents true (doubtless to the disappointment of thousands of aspiring young wizards and witches). We will look later at the reliability of the Gospels, and will also look specifically at some other parts of the New Testament. Here, we will consider briefly whether the reporting of the life, death, and resurrection of Jesus is something which purports to be based on first-hand evidence, or on hearsay evidence, or on rumour and story.

Quite simply, the New Testament account of Jesus purports to come directly from first-hand witnesses. Time and time again the early Christians stated "we are witnesses", and indeed the essential qualification for being an apostle was personal experience of Jesus' resurrection: when a new apostle was chosen to replace Judas, the "essential" and not simply "desirable" qualification for the post was "one of the men who have been with us the whole time the Lord Jesus was living among us, beginning from John's baptism to the time when Jesus was taken up from us. For one of these must become a witness with us of his resurrection" (Acts 1:21–22).

The word "witness" appears over and over again, for example in these extracts:

- God has raised this Jesus to life, and we are all witnesses of it (Acts 2:32).

- You killed the author of life, but God raised him from the dead. We are witnesses of this (Acts 3:15).

- The God of our ancestors raised Jesus from the dead – whom you killed by hanging him on a cross … we are witnesses of these things (Acts 5:30, 32).

- We are witnesses of everything he did… God raised him from the dead on the third day and caused him to be seen. He was not seen by all the people, but by witnesses whom God had already chosen (Acts 10:39–41).

- The man who saw it has given testimony, and his testimony is true (John 19:35).

- This is the disciple who testifies to these things and who wrote them down (John 21:24).

- For we did not follow cleverly devised stories when we told you about the coming of our Lord Jesus Christ in power, but we were eye-witnesses of his majesty (2 Peter 1:16).

- I appeal as a fellow elder and a witness of Christ's sufferings (1 Peter 5:1).

- (Possibly the most poetic of all:)"That which was from the beginning, which we have heard, which we have seen with our eyes, which we have looked at and our hands have touched… The life appeared; we have seen it and testify to it… We proclaim to you what we have seen and heard (1 John 1:1–3).

Even Luke, who makes it clear that he was *not* a witness to Jesus' life, goes on to make it equally clear that his information was derived from "those who from the first were eye-witnesses" (Luke 1:2). At the beginning of his second book he states, "After his suffering, he presented himself to them and gave many convincing proofs that he was alive" (Acts 1:3).

When Paul appeared before the Roman governor Festus, he said, "The king is familiar with these things … I am convinced that none of this has escaped his notice, because it was not done in a corner" (Acts 26:26). And to the church in Corinth he said that, if Jesus had not been raised from the dead, "we are then found to be false witnesses about God, for we have testified about God that he raised Christ from the dead" (1 Corinthians 15:15).

Many more examples could be given. The simple fact is that the New Testament purports to be written by people who were witnesses of the events reported or based on the testimony of such people. The language used, "witness" and "testimony", is unashamedly legal language, and appears to have been carefully chosen to add weight to what was being preached and then later written down. The authors were assuring their readers, who had not all witnessed the events, "These are genuine eye-witness accounts."

We will consider later whether such claims are accurate, but the inescapable conclusion is that the writers of the New Testament did not believe that they were writing myths, legends, or fairy stories. Nor were they simply writing abstract theology. They were recording evidence of actual events.

SUMMARY

- The number and age of New Testament manuscripts compares extremely favourably with other ancient texts.
- The writers of the New Testament wrote as, or reflecting the testimony of, eyewitnesses.

CHAPTER 5

The Judge

*I do swear by Almighty God that I will well and
truly serve our Sovereign Lady Queen Elizabeth the
Second in the office of … Judge, and I will do right to
all manner of people after the laws and usages of this
realm, without fear or favour, affection or ill will.*

The judicial oath

For centuries it has been a central principle of the English legal
system that *nemo debet esse judex in propria causa* – no one can
be judge in his own cause. The European Convention on Human
Rights provides, in Article 6, that "in the determination of his
civil rights and obligations or of any criminal charge against
him, everyone is entitled to a fair and public hearing within a
reasonable time by an independent and impartial tribunal". For
this reason from time to time judges have to determine whether
they should hear a particular case or whether they should
"recuse" themselves (as such self-removal is called) because
they have an actual or perceived interest in the case.

The principles to be applied were set out by the House
of Lords in the *Locabail* case (Locabail (UK) Ltd -v- Bayfield
Properties Ltd and Another [2000] 2 WLR 870) in which they
stated that, where a judge had an interest in the outcome of a
case, he would automatically be disqualified from hearing it;
and where there was a real possibility or danger of bias, a judge
should also recuse himself.

Obviously these rules do not apply to our day-to-day decision-making, as we do need to make decisions about matters involving ourselves. We do not need to recuse ourselves from considering the question of whether Jesus rose from the dead simply because we may have a personal interest in the answer to the question. However, the rules are helpful nonetheless, because they remind us of the need to consider whether we have any prejudices, conscious or subconscious. If we do, we can seek to eradicate them, or at the very least minimize them, as we consider the evidence. This is particularly important for someone who feels inclined to *reject* the account of Jesus' resurrection because, in the words of anatomist P. B. Medawar: "The human mind treats a new idea the same way the body treats a strange protein: it rejects it."[14]

This can lead to the state described as "cognitive dissonance", which describes the condition where someone experiences conflicting ideas simultaneously, and as a result seeks to alter one or more of the ideas so as to produce harmony. A good example is that given by Leon Festinger in his book *When Prophecy Fails* (1956, 2008), in which he actually coined the phrase "cognitive dissonance". This examined a cult which had been awaiting the destruction of the world by aliens on a particular date. When the date came and went, rather than abandoning their views in the light of the evidence, most members of the group concluded that the aliens had given the earth a second chance, and that the group should spread their message further. To put it in a more light-hearted way, "Do not adjust your mind, there is a fault in reality!"

In considering whether we have any prejudices about the resurrection of Jesus, there is again a very wide spectrum of views, and we can identify the two extremes and the centre of the spectrum.

"The Bible says it – I believe it"

At one extreme is the view held by many Christians that the Bible is completely true in every factual statement which it makes – it is inerrant. The Bible states that Jesus rose from the dead, and this is the beginning and end of the matter. Apparent inconsistencies between the Gospel accounts of the resurrection can simply be ignored on this basis, as all the accounts must be true and therefore must be capable of reconciliation even if we cannot be certain how that can be done; we must trust that in the fullness of time God will make such matters clear, and in the meantime we must exercise faith and refuse to doubt the biblical record. This view derives from biblical verses such as 2 Timothy 3:16 – "all Scripture is God-breathed and is useful for teaching, rebuking, correcting and training in righteousness".

It is not the function of this book to analyse this view. However, readers who hold it need to realize that it is a "prejudice" in that it will prejudge how they consider the evidence. Indeed, it will prevent them from considering the evidence at all in any meaningful sense. The vast majority of people will not accept the argument that "the Bible says it, so it must be true", and of course they may see this as a way of avoiding difficult questions about the biblical accounts. This view must therefore be set aside to enable an impartial consideration of the evidence. If that results in the conclusion that the evidence is weak, there is of course nothing to prevent the believer from reverting to the view that, despite this, Jesus rose from the dead because that is what the Bible says. That would be a statement of faith, however, rather than a conclusion from the evidence.

"It is not scientifically possible"

At the other extreme is the view that everything which exists is governed exclusively by the laws of science as they are currently understood. For many, this is tantamount to saying that God does not exist. Therefore if Jesus existed he must have been nothing more or less than a man, and he could not have risen from the dead because that would be scientifically impossible.

This view also acts as a prejudice, as it will prejudge how the evidence is considered. Therefore this also needs to be set aside to enable an impartial consideration of the evidence. If this results in the conclusion that the evidence is strong, there is nothing to prevent the sceptic from reverting to the view that, despite this, Jesus cannot have risen from the dead because that would simply be impossible. Once again, that would be a statement of faith, rather than a conclusion from the evidence.

Some readers may object to this being classified as a statement of faith, on the basis that such a view is supported by the laws of science, and this is very different from a view supported by a belief in an inerrant Bible. However, any decision to ignore the conclusions of evidence must be a step of faith, the only question being: faith in what?

Shades in-between

At the centre of the spectrum are those who have no preconceived view as to whether Jesus rose from the dead. They may never have considered the question, and may not even be aware that there is a question to be considered. They may or may not have read the Bible, but probably do not consider it to be a special or unique book. They may be open to the possibility of a "supernatural" dimension, but may be unsure whether that is something which can be observed in any way.

Between this central position and the views at either extreme are a whole range of views about Jesus. The important thing at this stage is that each reader stop to think about his or her own view, and then try to put that view to one side while considering the evidence. That should make possible a conclusion based on the evidence alone.

This is the process in which judges engage every day. They will often "prejudge" a case in the sense that they will form an initial view based on many factors – for example, how the case has been presented in the pre-trial documents, how the parties look and behave, and other considerations. The important skill is to be able to identify and then set aside these prejudices and to determine the case *on the evidence alone*. The relatively small number of successful appeals based on failure by judges to exercise this skill shows that it is possible to take this step.

So, before reading any further, it would be very worthwhile to pause here and ask yourself what your view is about Jesus and the resurrection. Are you certain that it did or did not happen? Are you uncertain or confused about it? Having identified your view, try consciously to set this to one side. And then read on. If at any time you find yourself reacting to what you read – "Can that really be right?" or "That's not what I've heard before" – then stop and ask whether it is your prejudice which is speaking. Follow the evidence, with an open mind about where you will end up. And enjoy the journey!

SUMMARY

- We need to identify and set aside any prejudices we have about Jesus.

- One such prejudice is simply to believe all that the Bible says.

- Another prejudice is that Jesus was simply an ordinary man.

PART 2
THE EVIDENCE

CHAPTER 6

Starting Point

The normal first step in resolving issues of primary fact is, I feel sure, to add to what is common ground between the parties … such facts as are shown to be incontrovertible… It is …worth bearing in mind, when vexatious conflicts of oral testimony arise, that these fall to be judged against the background not only of what the parties agree to have happened but also of what plainly did happen.

Lord Bingham of Cornhill[15]

Courts do not exist to decide hypothetical questions or to make abstract decisions of law. Their role is to apply the law to a given set of facts. Sometimes those facts will be agreed by the parties, but more often the court must decide what the relevant facts are, with two or more competing versions being offered by the parties.

The starting point is to establish what facts are agreed. Then they embark on a fact-finding exercise in relation to the disputed areas by considering the evidence presented. So, in a simple traffic accident case, it is usually agreed that two or more vehicles were travelling at the *locus in quo* – the scene of the event – and that they ended up with damage (although occasionally it is suggested by a driver that the other vehicle "came out of nowhere", which tends to suggest that the driver was not in fact paying attention to traffic). It is clear that, in the intervening moments *something happened*. It is the role of the court to decide just what that was, applying the burden and standard of proof (as we considered in Part 1).

In the same way, as we look at the evidence concerning the resurrection, we need to constantly remind ourselves of the starting point, namely that *something happened*. It is our task, as we look at the evidence, to try to find a satisfactory explanation for the known facts.

The *locus in quo*

The locus for our investigation is first-century Palestine, a small and relatively insignificant outpost of the Roman Empire. Since the conquest of this "promised land" under the leadership of Joshua, the Jewish people had been through a rollercoaster of victories and defeats, unity and civil war, autonomy and subjugation by their enemies.

At the close of the Old Testament writings, around 400 BC, the Medes and Persians controlled the Jews and had allowed some of them to return to Jerusalem – the Old Testament books of Ezra, Nehemiah, Haggai, Zechariah and Malachi were written during the period after the Persians became overlords of the Jews.

However, the Persian empire in turn was overthrown by the Greeks under Alexander the Great, who conquered Palestine in 332 BC. The fiercely monotheistic Jews were now exposed to Greek culture. Following the death of Alexander his kingdom was divided in three. Conflicts raged and in 198 BC Syria took control of Palestine. Before this, the Jews had been given much freedom, including that of religion. However, in 168 BC Antiochus IV of Syria took the title *Epiphanes* ("God-manifest") and sought to end Jewish religious observance and required the worship of other gods such as Zeus. This prompted the Maccabean revolt in which great victories were won and the temple was rededicated (commemorated to this day in the festival of Hanukkah).

After this the Hasmonean dynasty came to power and ruled until 63 BC, when the Roman general Pompey defeated the king, Aristobulus, and committed the ultimate desecration of entering the holy place in the temple. An unsuccessful rebellion followed, resulting in Herod the Great ruling as a puppet of the Roman Empire until his death in AD 4 when the "kingdom" was split between three of his sons. To cement their control of the land the Romans appointed procurators (governors) who took controversial steps including taking a census, imposing taxation and seizing part of the temple treasury. Inevitably this led to more rebellions, which were put down with great violence. At the time we are considering (around AD 30–33) Herod Antipas ruled Galilee, Philip ruled the north-eastern territories, and the Roman governor Pontius Pilate was procurator.

Despite this history of conquest by a series of world powers, the Jews held firm to their faith. They were the chosen people of God, living in the land promised to their ancestor Abraham. The epicentre of their faith was the temple in Jerusalem, in which the daily ritual of sacrifice was undertaken by the priests and Levites. Herod the Great had begun reconstruction of the temple in 20 BC, but the work was not finally completed until AD 63. The result was a truly magnificent building (see, for example, Mark 13:1). Although their Roman masters worshipped many gods, including emperor worship, the Jews held firmly to their belief in one God, stated clearly in the *Shema* prayer, "Hear, O Israel: the Lord our God, the Lord is One" (Deuteronomy 6:4). They maintained their rituals, their food laws and their festivals, and generally this was tolerated by the Romans.

Underlying all of this was the Jewish hope of a messiah, one from the line of King David who would overthrow their enemies and establish God's kingdom on earth, with Jerusalem as its capital and the dispersed people of Israel returned to the land. This expectation was clearly set out in the Psalms of Solomon, believed to have been written somewhere in the first century BC. Aspiring messiahs came and went, leaving little imprint on history. Some Jews (the Pharisees) sought to maintain the purity of their faith, while waiting for the Messiah; others (the Zealots, although that term may not have been used at the time) went further, and actively opposed the Romans. Yet others (the Sadducees) supported the status quo because of the power they enjoyed, and even collaborated with the Romans. Interestingly, according to the Gospels, Jesus had followers from all these groups – Nicodemus, a Pharisee (John 3:1); Simon, a zealot (Luke 6:15); Joseph of Arimathea, an influential member of the Jewish ruling council (Mark 15:43), and Matthew, also known as Levi, a tax collector (Matthew 9:9).

Finally, there was a widespread belief among the Jews that there would be a resurrection of the righteous dead at some point in the future, as part of the restoration of Israel. Not all Jews held that belief (the Sadducees did not, see for example Acts 23:8), but those who did believed not in anything esoteric such as a "spiritual resurrection" or the resurrection of the soul, but in something very concrete – that the resurrection would involve a new body.[16]

This, then is the *locus in quo* with which we must begin.

Result – the known facts

Something happened in this locus, which produced a result or effect. That result was, put simply, the early church. We will look later in more detail at their teaching and practice; at this stage we need only observe that from a very early stage the early Christians began to proclaim that:

- Although Jesus had died the death of a common criminal, he was nonetheless the Messiah eagerly awaited by the Jews.

- Although the Jews remained under the domination of the Romans, Jesus had nonetheless inaugurated the kingdom of God.

- Although Jesus had been a living, breathing, eating, weeping, man, he was nonetheless in some unique way God himself.

- Although the temple was still in operation (though only, as it turned out, for another forty years), Jesus was nonetheless the true temple, the true priest and the true sacrifice.

- Although Jesus had been dead and buried, he had then been raised to new life.

Our summary of the locus shows just how extraordinary this series of proclamations was. At a stroke it was blasphemy to the Jews and treachery to the Romans. It took the Jewish expectations of the Messiah, the kingdom of God and resurrection, and completely redefined them. And, against all the odds, it survived opposition and persecution and outlived the Jewish temple (destroyed by the Romans in AD 70), the Jewish state (the Jews were forbidden from entering what had been Jerusalem after AD 135) and the Roman Empire (the Western Empire is generally agreed to have ended in AD 476). The simple but profound question we must ask is this: what happened which was so powerful as to produce this result? We must continually bear this in mind as we work systematically through the evidence.

SUMMARY

- Despite Roman occupation, first-century Judaism remained monotheistic, centred on the temple, with a strong messianic hope.
- From this emerged the early church, which reinterpreted the fundamentals of Jewish belief.
- *Something unexpected happened* to produce this result.

CHAPTER 7

Paul

*I do not believe that it can be disputed that in the case
of the Apostle [Paul] we have the most powerful, most
conclusive evidence conceivable in forensic terms, of the
resurrection of our Lord, short of His actual return.*[17]

As we turn to the evidence, our first witness is the apostle Paul.
This may come as a surprise to many readers, who will expect
us to consider first the four New Testament Gospels. However,
there are a number of reasons why the evidence of Paul should
be considered first:

- There is considerable scholarly debate as to the
authorship of the Gospels. By contrast, there is strong
scholarly consensus that Paul wrote many, if not most,
of the New Testament letters attributed to him.

- It is generally agreed that the Gospels were written later
than Paul's letters.

- The Gospels are criticized by some as being
propaganda, designed to argue a case. By contrast,
Paul's letters are writings to groups of Christians. What
he has to say about Jesus tends to be incidental to the
points he is making.

- As we will see, there are apparent inconsistencies in
the Gospels. By contrast, Paul's writings are completely
consistent in their dealing with Jesus.

- Paul wrote a very significant proportion of the New Testament.

- We have an independent source of information about Paul – the book of Acts, with which we can compare his own writings.

Saul before

What do we know about Paul himself from his writings? He was clearly a devout, some might say fanatical, Jew. In his words he was "circumcised on the eighth day, of the people of Israel, of the tribe of Benjamin, a Hebrew of Hebrews; in regard to the law, a Pharisee; as for zeal, persecuting the church; as for righteousness based on the law, faultless" (Philippians 3:5–6). Again, "you have heard of my previous way of life in Judaism, how intensely I persecuted the church of God and tried to destroy it. I was advancing in Judaism beyond many of my own age among my people and was extremely zealous for the traditions of my fathers" (Galatians 1:13–14). In summary, he was "a persecutor and a violent man" (1 Timothy 1:13). This accords with what we read in Acts, that Paul (then called Saul) was present as a young man at the stoning of Stephen and "approved of their killing him", and after that he was "breathing out murderous threats against the Lord's disciples" (Acts 8:1; 9:1). Not exactly the obvious candidate to become a champion of the Christian faith!

A change of heart

How, then, did Paul come to change his views? Clearly something unexpected and dramatic happened – so what was that something? His letters show him to have an outstanding mind and a deep knowledge of the Jewish scriptures, so it is entirely plausible that study and reasoning played a part in his transformation. However, it is inherently unlikely that this alone would account for such a radical change.

Paul himself gives us an answer which is both remarkably simple and deeply profound: "Have I not seen Jesus our Lord?' (1 Corinthians 9:1). Indeed, he is at pains to point out that the good news (gospel) he preached came directly from Jesus – "the gospel I preached is not of human origin. I did not receive it from any man, nor was I taught it; rather, I received it by revelation from Jesus Christ" (Galatians 1:11–12).

Once again, this accords with what we read in Acts. Paul's experience on the road to Damascus is well known, and of course gave rise to another widely used phrase – a "Damascus road" experience. What is fascinating is how Acts relates this experience. There are three accounts. In the first we read that "suddenly a light from heaven flashed around him. He fell to the ground and heard a voice say to him, 'Saul, Saul, why do you persecute me?' 'Who are you, Lord?' Saul asked. 'I am Jesus, whom you are persecuting,' he replied" (Acts 9:3–5).

At first sight, this seems to contradict Paul's testimony, because it does not involve any *sight* of Jesus, only the *sound* of his voice. However, a few verses later Ananias, who we are told was sent by God to Saul says that "the Lord … *appeared* to you on the road as you were coming here". Later on Barnabas took Saul to the apostles and "told them how Saul on his journey had *seen* the Lord *and* that the Lord had spoken to him" (Acts 9:17, 27, emphasis mine). Finally, when Paul much later relates the story to King Agrippa, he records Jesus having said to him, "I have *appeared* to you to appoint you as a servant and as a witness of what you have *seen* and will *see* of me" (Acts 26:16, emphasis mine).

So there can be no real doubt that Paul claimed to have had

a direct encounter with Jesus, of the same type as the encounters of the other apostles. In fact he lists Jesus' other appearances and concludes "and last of all he appeared to me also, as to one abnormally born" (1 Corinthians 15:8).

Paul after

When we consider the dramatic change in Paul's life, it is reasonable to suppose that there would have to be an equally dramatic explanation for it. He went from persecuting Christians to enjoying fellowship with them. He went from seeking to destroy the Christian message to being one of its most powerful preachers. He went from prizing his background and achievements to considering them "garbage" (Philippians 3:8). And he went from a position of growing status and power to one of hardship and suffering.

This last point is of some importance. As we have seen and will see again, the early Christians' belief in the risen Jesus carried no privileges or advantages for them, but instead led to ostracism and even persecution. In Paul's case, he initially faced suspicion from other Christians because of his track record (see Acts 9:26). As he went on to travel around, preaching about Jesus, a regular pattern emerged – a pattern of opposition from loyal Jews, often resulting in threats, violence, arrests and near-riots. He mentions this persecution in a number of places, most eloquently in this list from 2 Corinthians 11 (verses 23–27):

> I have ... been in prison more frequently, been flogged
> more severely, and been exposed to death again and
> again. Five times I received from the Jews the forty
> lashes minus one. Three times I was beaten with
> rods, once I was pelted with stones, three times I was
> shipwrecked, I spent a night and a day in the open sea,
> I have been constantly on the move. I have been in

danger from rivers, in danger from bandits, in danger
from my fellow Jews, in danger from Gentiles; in danger
in the city, in danger in the country, in danger at sea;
and in danger from false believers. I have laboured and
toiled and have often gone without sleep; I have known
hunger and thirst and have often gone without food; I
have been cold and naked.

Some of his letters were written from prison. And finally, he
lost his life as a martyr for his faith. So there can be no serious
suggestion that Paul's conversion was triggered by any obvious
benefit to himself.

Paul's testimony about the resurrection

So much for what Paul said about himself. What did he say
about Jesus? He is consistent throughout all the letters attributed
to him, and this is summarized in a well-known passage in 1
Corinthians 15 (verses 3–5):

For what I received I passed on to you as of first
importance: that Christ died for our sins according to
the Scriptures, that he was buried, that he was raised on
the third day according to the Scriptures, and that he
appeared…

Put more simply, and stripping out the theological elements of
this statement, Paul says that:

• Jesus died and was buried, and

• Jesus rose from the dead and appeared.

Paul says that this was passed on to him (presumably by other
Christians, or by Jesus) and that he had then passed it on to the

Corinthian Christians. This basic teaching is repeated time and again throughout Paul's letters. For example:

- Romans – "Christ Jesus who died – more than that, who was raised to life" (Romans 8:34).

- 2 Corinthians – "he was crucified in weakness, yet he lives by God's power" (2 Corinthians 13:4).

- Galatians – "God the Father, who raised [Jesus Christ] from the dead"; "before your very eyes Christ was clearly portrayed as crucified" (Galatians 1:1; 3:1).

- Ephesians – "when [God] raised [Christ] from the dead"; "to reconcile both of them to God through the cross" (Ephesians 1:20; 2:16).

- Philippians – "he humbled himself by becoming obedient to death – even death on a cross"; "I want to know Christ – yes, to know the power of his resurrection" (Philippians 2:8; 3:10).

- Colossians – "making peace through his blood, shed on the cross"; "he has reconciled you by Christ's physical body through death"; "faith in the working of God, who raised him from the dead" (Colossians 1:20, 22; 2:12).

- 1 Thessalonians – "We believe that Jesus died and rose again" (1 Thessalonians 4:14).

It is abundantly clear that Paul's belief in the physical death and resurrection of Jesus was at the very heart of his faith and teaching. With the exception of the "formulaic" presentation of this basic belief in 1 Corinthians, he tends to mention it in passing, to reinforce points which he is making. He is therefore presupposing that his readers will be thoroughly aware of it. This is entirely consistent with the record of his preaching in Acts, where he invariably focuses on the death and resurrection of Jesus.

In addition, Paul refers in passing to other elements of the "passion" story (the accounts of Christ's suffering). He refers to Jesus making a "good confession" while "testifying before Pontius Pilate" (1 Timothy 6:13), and he refers in detail to the last supper, again saying, "I received from the Lord what I also passed on to you" (1 Corinthians 11:23). As before, he assumes that his readers are familiar with these incidents, and refers to them as part of points which he is making.

Paul's theology

Paul's belief in the death and resurrection of Jesus forms the bedrock of his theology. This book is not the place to consider Paul's theology in any detail, but it is important to note that without the death and resurrection of Jesus, Paul would essentially have no theology! At every point his theological arguments are based squarely on these beliefs.

For example, throughout the dense theological arguments of Romans runs the simple proposition that people can be justified because of Jesus' death and resurrection: "He was delivered over to death for our sins and was raised to life for our justification" (Romans 4:25).[18] And in a powerful passage in 1 Corinthians 15 he argues forcefully that if Jesus was not raised from the dead, then no one would be raised from the dead, and so "your faith is futile", "our preaching is useless" and "we are then found to be false witnesses about God". But he concludes that "Christ has indeed been raised from the dead, the firstfruits of those who have fallen asleep" (see 1 Corinthians 15:12–20).

It is abundantly clear, then, that Paul believed he had met the risen Christ. He had an experience which utterly transformed his life and his worldview. He moved from orthodox Jewish views to a theology based on the physical death and resurrection of Jesus. He went from a position of some status and power to one of persecution and ultimately death. This is explained perfectly by his new beliefs: as he says in Romans 8:18, "I consider that our present sufferings are not worth comparing with the glory that will be revealed in us."

A barrister's conclusion

We conclude our examination of Paul's testimony where we started, with an incisive commentary by barrister Roger Gray:

> I address this point by asking if there is any way of infallibly proving a disputed case to a jury beyond reasonable doubt. Within the limits of human perfection I think there is, but it would need some arranging. If I were asked to arrange such a case I would arrange it thus: First I would identify not just the world's, but history's leading expert on the disputed point in my case. I would arrange that he was acknowledged to be one of the most brilliant minds in history, and that he was acknowledged to be the leading authority on the disputed point. I would arrange for him to be a witness against my case. I would arrange for him to be so hostile to my case and to hate it with such a fierce and total dedication that he assassinated at least one of my witnesses, had others imprisoned, and wished to continue doing so. I would arrange for him to have high social prestige. I would have him supported by the entire legal, political, social, and religious establishment of the day, and I would have him understand that

the continuation of this support and social esteem depended absolutely in his maintaining his opinion, so that he could not deviate from his position except in the most degrading and disgraceful terms. I would then have him publicly repudiate his own position and concede in the most humiliating terms that his own case was wrong, and that my case was right, knowing that in doing so he was destroying his own reputation and position without hope of rehabilitation. I cannot conceive of any circumstances where more powerful or compelling evidence could be given than this. If these circumstances were replicated, any trial lawyer will tell you that it would take a jury about a millisecond to decide that the case was proved without any doubt whatsoever. In this light I would then ask anyone to consider the career of the Apostle Paul.[19]

But of course it remains possible that Paul was honestly yet gravely mistaken. As Governor Festus is reported as saying to him: "Your great learning is driving you insane" (Acts 26:24). We need to move on to consider the next witness.

SUMMARY

- Paul was a devout Jew, involved in persecuting Christians.
- Something unexpected happened to change him into a Christian preacher, theologian, missionary and martyr.
- Both he and the writer of Acts attributed the change to seeing the risen Jesus.

CHAPTER 8

James

I sought my soul, but my soul I could not see. I sought my God, but my God eluded me. I sought my brother and I found all three.

Author unknown

Our second witness is James, the brother of Jesus, and he could not be more different from Paul. Paul is widely accepted as being the author of many letters – the largest proportion of the New Testament attributed to a single author. In contrast, only one short letter is attributed to James, and there is disagreement among scholars as to whether he was even the author of that. Martin Luther once famously described his letter as "a right strawy epistle" in comparison with the letters of Paul and others! Even if James was the author of the letter bearing his name, unlike Paul's letters it contains no biographical information at all. The rest of the New Testament also contains very little biographical information about him – unlike Paul. In particular, there is no detailed account of his conversion to the cause of Christ.

What we do know about James is limited to some passing descriptions about Jesus' family in general, a number of references to James' role in the early church, a pregnant question as to what happened in-between the two, and a tantalizing brief reference which provides the only probable answer to that question. We will look at each in turn.

James before

We consider first the role of James during Jesus' lifetime, and immediately we discover a paradox. As we will see, James had a very prominent role in the early church, yet he is only mentioned by name in passing in the Gospels (Matthew 13:55; Mark 6:3). If we had no other information, we would most probably conclude that he played no significant part before Jesus died. However, we do have some information about Jesus' family in general, and there is every reason to think that this included James. And it seems, far from supporting Jesus' ministry, his family were clearly very puzzled about it, and even tried to stop him: "For even his own brothers did not believe in him" (John 7:5). "When his family heard about this, they went to take charge of him, for they said, 'He is out of his mind'" (Mark 3:21).

When teaching in his home town, Jesus is recorded as not doing many miracles there "because of their lack of faith". This is a reference to the people of the town generally, rather than to Jesus' family, but his comments are telling: "A prophet is not without honour except in his own town *and in his own home*" (Matthew 13:57–58 emphasis mine).

Given James' later prominence in the church, it is highly unlikely that this information would have been included in the Gospels unless it were true. There is no other reason why the writers of the Gospels would have included stories which showed the early disbelief of one of its leaders. If James' attitude had been any different to that of the rest of the family, then he would have been mentioned by name, in the same way as the Gospels often distinguish between different disciples. The only conclusion that is possible is that James, Jesus' own brother, did not believe in what he was doing during Jesus' lifetime. We can only speculate how difficult Jesus must have found the disbelief and lack of support of his own family. And in fact, when he was told that his family were arriving, he responded, "Who are my mother and my brothers?... Whoever does God's will is my brother and sister and mother" (Mark 3:31–35) – a surprisingly non-family-friendly response!

James after

In the light of this conclusion, it is nothing short of astonishing to discover that James rapidly became one of the prominent leaders of the early church. He is mentioned frequently in the book of Acts, which is particularly significant because Acts was written by the same author as the Gospel of Luke, which does not mention James at all. James is first mentioned in Acts 12 when Peter, having been miraculously released from prison, says, "Tell James and the other brothers and sisters about this" (Acts 12:17).[20] This suggests that James already had a position of some authority, and this is made explicit in chapter 15 when, at a meeting of the "apostles and elders" it was James who responded to what Paul and Barnabas said and who concluded with the words "It is my judgment..." (Acts 15:6, 13–21). Indeed, Paul refers to James being known as a "pillar" of the church, together with Peter and John (Galatians 2:9).

Not only was James a leader of the early church but, as we shall see later on, he paid for his faith with martyrdom. This leaves us with a pregnant question: what happened to change James from someone who did not believe in what Jesus was doing during his lifetime, to someone who became totally committed to the early church after Jesus' death, a church which proclaimed openly precisely what James had doubted previously. What happened that could have produced such a complete transformation?

This was certainly not a transformation which produced an easy life or material benefit for James. The early church did not pay fat stipends to its leaders, and they were not respected outside the church. Persecution started very early on, and church leaders were particularly vulnerable.

Explaining the transformation

For an answer, we need to turn to our intriguing brief reference to James, found in one of Paul's letters. In 1 Corinthians 15 Paul lists the post-resurrection appearances of Jesus, and includes these words: "Then he appeared to James" (verse 7). That's it – the only reference that we have to any sort of conversion experience which James may have had. No detail, unlike the detail about Paul's conversion. No context, unlike the accounts in the Gospels of the appearances to the disciples. Just these few words. But those few words provide the most likely explanation for the transformation in James. And Paul was in a very good position to know about such an experience; as he explains in his letter to the Galatians, James was one of the two church leaders whom he met when he first returned to Jerusalem after his own conversion. While we do not have the sort of full explanation which we would ideally want, and while we have all manner of loose ends, the appearance of the risen Jesus to James really does provide the only plausible explanation for the fundamental change in James' life.

SUMMARY

- James, Jesus' brother, was sceptical about Jesus during his lifetime.

- Something unexpected happened which led him to become a leader of the early church and a martyr for his faith.

- The only plausible explanation for this change is that given by Paul – James had an experience of the risen Jesus.

CHAPTER 9

Peter

I have prayed for you, Simon, that your faith may not fail. And when you have turned back, strengthen your brothers.

Luke 22:32

Our next witness is Simon who was renamed Peter, and once again he is very different from our previous witnesses. Unlike James who was sceptical, and Paul who opposed the early Christians, Peter was a follower of Jesus from the beginning. In the Gospels we have no mention at all of Paul, a few passing references to James, but a wealth of information about Peter.

As Peter was such an early disciple, it might be thought that his value as a witness is much less than that of Paul or James – after all, he was already fully committed to Jesus' ministry, and was therefore much more likely to refuse to accept that the ministry had ended with Jesus' death. So in order to evaluate his role as a witness, it is necessary to look at what we know about Peter.

Given the issues that we have already briefly identified in relation to the reliability of the Gospels, we are treating their content with some caution. However, in the case of Peter there is a strong likelihood that their content is accurate. This is because the picture which they paint of Peter is not exactly flattering! Let us look at some specific instances.

Walking on water (or not!)

In Matthew 14:25–31 the disciples were rowing a boat across Galilee when Jesus approached them, walking on the water. The disciples were, not surprisingly, afraid. It was Peter who said, "Lord, if it's you, tell me to come to you on the water." Jesus did so, and Peter stepped out. However, when he saw the wind, he was afraid and began to sink. Jesus rebuked him, calling him a man of little faith! While the early church may well have invented a story of their leader Peter walking on water, they certainly would not invent a story which included him sinking and being rebuked by Jesus for his lack of faith.

Speaking without thinking

Matthew, Mark, and Luke all record the "transfiguration" in which, on a mountaintop, Jesus' clothes became dazzling white, and Elijah and Moses appeared (Matthew 17: 1–9; Mark 9:2–10; Luke 9:28–36). Peter, James and John were there, and were terrified. It was Peter who spoke, with the frankly silly suggestion, "Let us put up three shelters – one for you, one for Moses and one for Elijah." Mark and Luke both comment that Peter "did not know what he was saying", but that did not prevent him saying it!

Another rebuke

On one occasion (Matthew 16:13–23; Mark 8:27–33) Jesus asked his disciples, "Who do people say I am?" and they gave various answers. "Who do you say I am?" Jesus continued, and Peter answered, "You are the Messiah." Well done Peter, we might think, this time you've got it right! However, Jesus went on to say that he was going to suffer, be rejected and killed, and

Peter was having none of it, saying, "This shall never happen to you!" This led to a forceful rebuke by Jesus – "Get behind me, Satan! You are a stumbling-block to me; you do not have in mind the concerns of God, but merely human concerns." Again, it is very difficult to believe that the early church would invent a story in which their leader appeared to oppose Jesus and was rebuked in such shocking terms.

Refusing Jesus' love

John tells us that Jesus showed the disciples "the full extent of his love" when he washed their feet (John 13:1–10). It appears that all of the disciples accepted this display of love without demur… except of course Peter, who refused to let Jesus wash his feet. When Jesus said, "Unless I wash you, you have no part with me," Peter immediately went to the other extreme, inviting Jesus to wash his head and hands as well. We can only imagine Jesus sighing and thinking "here we go again" as he calmly explained that "those who have had a bath need only to wash their feet" (which would be dirty from the dusty roads).

Sleeping on duty

In the garden of Gethsemane Jesus asked Peter, James and John to keep watch while he prayed. He found them asleep. Both Matthew and Mark record that Jesus said specifically to Peter, "Couldn't you keep watch for one hour? Watch and pray so that you will not fall into temptation. The spirit is willing, but the flesh is weak" (Mark 14:37–38). This is another episode which Peter would not have been proud of, and which the early church would not have made up.

Arguing with Jesus

Jesus predicted that his disciples would abandon him. As we have come to expect, Peter would not accept this. "Even if all fall away, I will not." He probably wished he had said nothing, as Jesus went on to say that Peter would deny him three times. Again Peter protested, "Even if I have to die with you, I will never disown you" (Mark 14:29–31). [21]

Denying Jesus

This is a very well-known aspect of the events leading to Jesus' death. (Each of the four Gospels contains a record of it: Matthew 26:69–75; Mark 14:66–72; Luke 22:54–62; John 18:15–18, 25–27.) As predicted by Jesus – and vehemently rejected by Peter – he did go on to deny knowing Jesus three times. This included a denial to a servant girl, when Peter even "began to call down curses, and he swore to them, 'I don't know the man!'" When he realized what he had done, he broke down and wept. Peter's actions are all the more surprising as he had earlier drawn his sword to prevent Jesus' arrest (John 18:10).

So we see that Peter is consistently portrayed as someone who speaks before he thinks, who lacks understanding and faith, and who despite all his bravado ultimately was too afraid even to admit to a servant girl that he knew Jesus, denying his friend and master instead. This is not the sort of information that a major leader of the church would want in the public domain. In our time it is the sort that a celebrity would try to cover up by threatening libel proceedings. However, "justification" (that the words written are true) is a full defence to libel proceedings, and these comments about Peter are highly likely to be in the

Gospels because they were already public knowledge in the church – because they were true. They do not paint a picture of someone likely to go on to become a great leader and bold preacher – unless something very significant happened.

And what do we find? According to the book of Acts, from the very beginning of the public preaching by the first Christians it was Peter who took the lead (Acts 1:15; 2:14–41). He was soon arrested. His bold defence of his actions before the Sanhedrin (the Jewish ruling council) could not have been a starker contrast to his denial only a few weeks earlier (Acts 4:1–21). Acts, Paul's letters and the later writings of early church "fathers" such as Clement, Irenaeus and Tertullian all confirm that Peter was one of the main leaders of the early church. There is also a very strong tradition, referred to by many of the "fathers", that Peter was eventually crucified upside down, around AD 64–65 during the persecution of Christians by the infamous Emperor Nero.

As with James, we are given a very clear explanation of what happened to change Peter's life – he met the risen Jesus. Paul tells us this in 1 Corinthians 15:5. As we will see, John is the only Gospel to record a specific meeting between Jesus and Peter, when Peter is reinstated. However, all four Gospels record Jesus appearing to the eleven disciples, and the opening words of the book of 1 Peter (thought by most scholars to have been written by Peter himself, or at his direction) proclaim praise to God who "has given us new birth into a living hope through the resurrection of Jesus Christ from the dead" (1 Peter 1:3).

So there are several independent sources confirming that Peter met the risen Jesus. Even if we did not have those sources, we would have to think long and hard for another explanation of the significant change which Peter underwent.

SUMMARY

- The Gospel records show Peter as someone who lacked understanding and faith, and who denied Jesus.

- Something unexpected happened which resulted in him becoming a major leader and preacher in the early church, who died for his faith in Jesus.

- There are several sources indicating that he changed by meeting the risen Jesus.

CHAPTER 10

No Body

*Now it is perfectly clear that there is apparently no
reported case in English law where a man has been
convicted of murder when there has been no trace of the
body at all. But it is equally clear that the fact of death,
like any other fact, can be proved by circumstantial
evidence, that is to say, evidence of facts which lead to
one conclusion, provided that the jury are satisfied and
are warned that it must lead to one conclusion only.*

Lord Goddard, Lord Chief Justice[22]

Huge academic and popular interest was generated in February
2013 when DNA testing established that a skeleton buried
under a car park in Leicester was that of King Richard III. The
lead archaeologist, Richard Buckley of Leicester University,
used exactly the same legal language as we are using in this
book when he announced that "beyond reasonable doubt it's
Richard".[23]

This contrasted starkly with an attempt by the Parish
of Holy Trinity Bosham to investigate two grave sites in the
nave of the church as "part of a substantial, serious, and not
sensational, television programme about the death and burial"
of King Harold. Chancellor Hill, the judge presiding over the
case in the Chichester Consistory Court, concluded that

> whilst I am sympathetic to the continuing quest for
> knowledge concerning our nation's history, the prospect

of obtaining a meaningful result is so remote in this instance that the presumption against disturbance [of the bodies] is not displaced. The evidence led by the petitioners fails to come near to the standard required.

Re Holy Trinity, Bosham [2004] 2 AER 820, at page 832

Identifying the remains of important figures from history generates highly significant evidence, particularly where there are questions to be answered about how they died or whether they were related to specific individuals.

In 2007 Channel 4 screened a controversial documentary, *The Lost Tomb of Jesus*. The executive producer was James Cameron, the director of the cinematic blockbusters *Titanic* and *Avatar*. The documentary told the story of the discovery of the "Talpiot tomb" in Jerusalem (so named because it is located in the East Talpiot area). The tomb, originally excavated in 1980 when it was discovered by workmen, contained ten ossuaries (bone boxes), seven of which bore inscriptions. It was claimed that these inscriptions identified Jesus, his mother Mary, his brothers Joseph and James, his wife Mary Magdalene, his son Judah, and Matthew. Statistically, it was said, the chance of finding these names together in a tomb but relating to someone other than the biblical Jesus was somewhere between 600 to 1 and 1 million to 1. The programme makers denied that their findings contradicted orthodox Christian teaching.

Since the screening of the documentary, experts of all relevant disciplines have queued up to refute the claims. Historians, palaeographers and archaeologists have disputed the identification of the names on the ossuaries with the biblical characters. Statisticians have pointed out that the figures produced are based on assumptions (that the names are those of the biblical characters, that Jesus was married to Mary, and so on) and that without those assumptions, the chance of the tomb being that of Jesus' family is very remote. Amos Kloner, the area supervisor for the Israel Department of Antiquities at the time of the excavation, said to the *Jerusalem Post*, "It makes a great story for a TV film, but it's completely impossible. It's nonsense." François Bovon, one of the experts interviewed in the programme, said that he was only asked about a particular issue and was not aware of the nature of the whole programme. In a letter to the Society of Biblical Literature (available on their website) he described the reconstructions of Jesus' marriage to Mary as belonging "to science fiction".

Details of some of the main criticisms of the "evidence" presented in the programme are listed in Appendix 2. A fair consideration of that evidence would suggest that the conclusions reached bear as much resemblance to history as does the story of Rose and Jack in *Titanic* (which was a fictional device even though the film was based on actual historical events).

The reason why the programme was possible, and why its conclusions were so controversial, is that Jesus' body has never been found. Indeed, there is no actual certainty about where he was buried. There are two "rival" sites in Jerusalem, one within the Church of the Holy Sepulchre and the other known as the Garden Tomb. The Holy Sepulchre was built by Emperor Constantine in AD 326–330, although it has been destroyed and rebuilt more than once since then. It was built on the site of a temple to the goddess Venus, which had been built by Emperor Hadrian around AD 135. The Christian historian Eusebius, who was a contemporary of Constantine, claimed in his *Life of Constantine* that worship services had been held at the site (which is said to include Golgotha, the place of Jesus' crucifixion) until AD 66, when Jerusalem was captured by the Romans, although it is not clear from where he obtained that information. The Garden Tomb was discovered by General

Gordon in 1867, and there is little to suggest that it was the tomb of Jesus. The Oxford Archaeological Guide to the Holy Land concludes that the Holy Sepulchre church "very probably" is the place where Jesus died and was buried.

Other locations have been suggested. Perhaps the most surprising is the Roza Bal tomb in Kashmir, India. Officially, it is the tomb of Youza Asaph, a medieval Muslim preacher. However some claim that it is actually Jesus who is buried there, and this theory is advanced in the tombofjesus.com website. The evidence produced there is nothing more than speculation (for instance, that Jesus did not die on the cross and that travel to India would have been possible[24]), and a BBC correspondent has commented that "professional historians tend to laugh out loud when you mention the notion that Jesus may have lived in Kashmir".[25] That has not stopped popular writers advancing the theory, for example Sylvia Browne in *The Mystical Life of Jesus,* subtitled "An Uncommon Perspective on the Life of Christ", her main source of information being a spirit guide named Francine.

The uncertainty about the location of Jesus' tomb is in stark contrast to the tombs of other significant religious leaders. There is no doubt that Muhammad's tomb is located in the "Prophet's Mosque" (Al-Masjid al-Nabawi) in Medina, or that Abraham is buried in the "Cave of Patriarchs" (Machpelah) in Hebron. Confucius is buried in the Kong Lin cemetery in his home town of Qufu, China. It is not disputed that the body of the Buddha was cremated and the ashes were buried beneath monuments ("stupas"). The only exception is Guru Nanak, the founder of Sikhism, whose body disappeared after his death. And although there was a dispute between his followers as to how his body should be disposed of, there is no dispute about where the body lay.

In simple terms, it is quite extraordinary that there is no certainty about the tomb of Jesus, the founder of one of the world's largest religions. This uncertainty is all the more surprising when it is understood that Jewish burial was a two-stage process, the second being the placing of the bones in an ossuary after the body had decomposed. It would be unthinkable to have carried out the first stage but to show no interest whatsoever in the second. The simple and obvious explanation for this was that the early Christians had no particular interest in the tomb. Despite what Eusebius says, there is no mention in the New Testament or other early Christian writings of its location, which is particularly surprising given that the Gospels clearly state that observers saw "where he was laid" (Mark 15:47; see also Matthew 27:61; Luke 23:55). Again, there is a simple and obvious explanation for this lack of interest; once the tomb was found to be empty and the disciples experienced the risen Jesus, there was no reason for them to pay any further attention to the tomb, and no need to consider the second stage of burial.

In fact, in the first recorded sermon of the early church, Peter drew a stark comparison between "the patriarch David" who "died and was buried, and his tomb is here to this day", and Jesus who "was not abandoned to the realm of the dead, nor did his body see decay" (Acts 2:29–31). The Jews knew all about the importance of preserving the tombs of their leaders, but there never seems to have been any question of the early Christians (who were all from a Jewish background) doing the same for the tomb of Jesus.

The absence of Jesus' body and the lack of any interest in his tomb are entirely consistent with the claim that Jesus rose from the dead. Indeed, that is precisely why claims such as those made in *The Lost Tomb of Jesus* are taken so seriously by Christians. Despite what was said by the programme makers, the discovery of Jesus' body would be irrefutable evidence that he did not rise from the dead in any physical sense. While this would not exclude the idea of a "spiritual" resurrection, that is clearly not what the writers of the New Testament were talking about when they wrote about an empty tomb, an absent body and physical appearances.

Some other explanations of the lack of Jesus' body have been suggested, and we will consider these in a later chapter. However, at this stage we should simply note that the pieces of "real evidence" which we would usually expect to find (a body and a grave) are, respectively, missing and uncertain.

SUMMARY

- Despite claims to the contrary, there is no certainty about the location of Jesus' tomb, and his body is missing; this contrasts with other significant religious leaders.

- *Something unexpected happened* which meant that these questions were of no interest to the early church.

- The obvious explanation of this is their belief that Jesus had risen from the dead.

CHAPTER 11

The Early Church

*The birth and rapid rise of the Christian Church...
remain an unsolved enigma for any historian who
refuses to take seriously the only explanation offered by
the Church itself.*

C. F. D. Moule (1967), page 13

When you think no one is watching you

In the vast majority of civil trials, judges make decisions based on evidence given honestly by witnesses. However, a not insignificant number of claims are brought fraudulently, and recent years have seen a number of convictions of individuals who have brought false claims (particularly arising from "staged" traffic accidents). In other cases, part of the claim is genuine, but it is exaggerated so as to increase the amount of damages. In 2012 the Supreme Court confirmed that in exceptional cases, a claimant's entire claim could be struck-out where it was exaggerated (Fairclough Homes -v- Summers [2012] UKSC 26).

In that case, the claimant Mr Summers had suffered fractures to his right hand and his left heel. He had claimed damages of over £800,000 but recovered only £88,716. His exaggeration was unmasked by the use of video surveillance, which is used in an increasing number of cases. The court stated that "what is seen on the video tapes is absolutely inconsistent with such disabilities". For example, the videos showed Mr Summers using crutches when entering and leaving doctors' surgeries, but not using them when leaving and returning home before and after these examinations. In fact, the Supreme Court did not consider this to be an exceptional case, so Mr Summers was able to retain his award of £88,716.

The important point raised by such cases is that it may be necessary to consider not just the direct evidence given by a party, but also whether his words and actions outside court are consistent with his evidence. So far, we have identified that something unexpected happened which led to the creation and growth of the early church. We have considered specifically the lives and writings of Paul, James, and Peter, and the lack of interest by the early church in the location of Jesus' tomb. What other evidence is there about the early church which may assist us as we consider the question of what actually happened?

Then and now

The church in the twenty-first century extends throughout the entire world; by some estimates a third of the world's population would describe themselves as Christian. It has come a very long way from the relatively obscure Roman province where it began. Although many point to the conversion of Emperor Constantine in AD 312 as the real beginning of the growth of the church, the reality is that Christianity was widespread both geographically and socially at least a century before this, and Constantine did not make it either the official or the exclusive religion of the Roman Empire. Professor Chadwick in *The Early Church* (page 71) comments:

> The faith of a handful of ill-educated fishermen had
> spread with astonishing rapidity to reach from India to
> Mauretania, from the Caspian to the utterly barbarous

tribes of Britain. The agents of this diffusion had not
been great orators or subtle reasoners, and they had had
to meet the opposition of prejudiced and angry mobs
and of a hostile government. Nevertheless, the churches
had expanded with extraordinary and embarrassing
speed.

This early growth was not accompanied by any military
conquest or territorial claims, or by pursuing a particular
political agenda. Unlike any religion before, it spread rapidly
through different races and political classes. Although the
earliest Christians were all Jews, the Christian faith rapidly
spread to "the Gentiles" – the other peoples and nations of the
world. At a very early stage Paul wrote, "There is neither Jew
nor Gentile, slave nor free, nor is there male and female, for you
are all one in Christ Jesus" (Galatians 3:28).

Unlike virtually every other religion and cult in history,
the church did not grow dramatically while its "founder" was
alive. It is widely accepted that Jesus died in his early thirties,
having exercised a public ministry for only three years.
Although thousands are said to have listened to his teaching,
his committed followers seemed to be numbered in hundreds
when he died (in 1 Corinthians 15, Paul records Jesus appearing
to "more than five hundred"; in Acts 1 the author refers to a
group of around one hundred and twenty believers). There is
no record of Jesus ever committing his teaching to writing.

How, then, are we to account for the birth and growth of
the early church? We have already considered its birthplace,
Palestine, ruled by Rome yet fiercely nationalistic and
monotheistic. We now need to look more carefully at some of
the characteristics of the early church.

The preaching of the early church

From the very beginning Christianity was a missionary faith – the Christians set out to tell others about what they believed, and to seek to persuade others to join them in those beliefs (see John 1:40–46 as the earliest example of this). Later on, after Jesus had gone, the death and resurrection of Jesus was at the very centre of their preaching. We have already seen how references to the resurrection appear in almost all of the letters thought to have been written by Paul. In addition, the numerous "sermons" and other proclamations recorded in Acts inevitably focus on Jesus' death and resurrection – "God raised him from the dead" is the constant refrain.[26] The early Christians were clearly aware of Jesus' teaching and the way he had lived his life, but these were not the focus of their preaching. Whatever else they believed, it is obvious that Jesus' death and resurrection formed the bedrock of their faith and therefore of their preaching. Although Christianity has always had a powerful message of love – God's love for people and the love that people should show to each other – that love was presented by the early church in the context of Jesus' death and resurrection. The resurrection was never an afterthought or a peripheral doctrine, but was always the essential basis of the belief of the early church. Indeed, belief in Jesus' resurrection is presented as an essential requirement of salvation: "If you declare with your mouth, 'Jesus is Lord,' and believe in your heart that God raised him from the dead, you will be saved" (Romans 10:9).

The death and resurrection of Jesus are always linked in the preaching of the early church. This is particularly telling because much of their theology could have been based solely on his death, which raises the question why the church insisted so strongly on the truth of the resurrection. Jesus' death was a known fact – it could be debated theologically, but it could not be disputed. Why did the early church insist on proclaiming the resurrection as well, when that could be disputed? This would be the same as adding to the detail of an accident claim a key detail which could be hotly disputed and which was not actually necessary for the success of the claim. There would be no reason for witnesses to insist upon such detail – unless it was true.

We also see the centrality of the resurrection in the way in which the beliefs of the church developed as the early Christians contemplated recent events in the light of their scriptures.

- They proclaimed that Jesus was the Messiah eagerly awaited by the Jews. Jesus in no way fitted the "job description" of the expected Messiah, who was expected to free the Jews from their pagan oppressors. Worse than this, he had been put to death as a criminal and, as such, was thought to have been under God's curse (Deuteronomy 21:23). Despite this, Jesus' disciples had the audacity to proclaim to their fellow Jews that "God has made this Jesus, whom you crucified, both Lord and Messiah" (Acts 2:36).

- Closely related to this, they proclaimed that Jesus had inaugurated the rule of the kingdom of God, even though to all intents and purposes nothing had changed. The Romans were still in control. However, the early church saw Jesus as the true Lord, ruling in a spiritual rather than a geographical kingdom – "he has rescued us from the dominion of darkness and brought us into the kingdom of the Son he loves" (Colossians 1:13). In Jesus people could experience eternal life, and that life began immediately – they could experience "new birth into a living hope through the resurrection of Jesus Christ from the dead" (1 Peter 1:3).

- Further, they began tentatively to suggest that Jesus was, in some unique way, God himself, which was blasphemy to the monotheistic Jews. They described Jesus as "the image of the invisible God" (Colossians 1:15), "in very nature God" (Philippians 2:6).

- They firmly believed that Jesus would return – "in the same way you have seen him go into heaven" (Acts 1:11).

It must be remembered that the New Testament is not a systematic handbook of theology, neatly divided into chapters dealing with each belief of the church. Rather, it contains theology worked out in the practical issues with which the church had to deal – its relationship with Judaism (was it necessary to be circumcised? was it permissible to consume blood?) and its relationship with other religions (was it permissible to eat meat sacrificed to idols?), to name but two areas.

But at the very heart of it all, standing as the foundation upon which everything else rests, is the teaching that Jesus died and rose again.

The practice of the early church

Among the distinctive practices of the early church, three stand out – the Lord's Supper, the Lord's Day, and baptism.

The Lord's Supper does not relate directly to the resurrection, although Paul states that partaking in the bread and wine proclaims the Lord's death "until he comes" (1 Corinthians 11:26). However, by the early second century the Lord's Supper was a regular part of the Christian meeting on the "Lord's Day". This was Sunday, the day on which Jesus was believed to have risen from the dead. Although there is no suggestion anywhere in the Gospels or elsewhere that Jesus instructed his followers to meet on that day, they started to meet to worship and remember his resurrection very early in the life of the church. Professor Chadwick (1967, 1993) comments (pages 128, 251) that this was traditional before Paul wrote 1 Corinthians (around AD 55). Although Sunday did not replace the Jewish sabbath as a day of rest until the fourth century, it was clearly celebrated from very early on in the life of the church.

Baptism was not unfamiliar to Judaism, and John the Baptist had been baptizing before the start of Jesus' ministry. Jesus was believed to have commanded his disciples to baptize after he had been raised from the dead (Matthew 28:19), and the early church rapidly linked this directly to his death and resurrection – Paul refers to baptism as being a spiritual circumcision, "having been buried with him in baptism, in which you were also raised with him through your faith in the working of God, who raised him from the dead" (Colossians 2:12).

So the distinctive practices of the early church were linked directly to Jesus' death and resurrection.

The persecution of the church

We have already seen how Peter, Paul, and James were put to death because of their faith. According to tradition all of the apostles except John (but including Matthias who took the place of Judas) were put to death as martyrs.[27] The early Christians faced persecution from both the Jews and the Romans. For the Jews their teachings were blasphemous, and according to Acts 7 and 8 Stephen was the first Christian to be killed, following which "a great persecution broke out against the church". For the Romans Christianity involved a number of issues which from time to time led to persecution and execution, including: the obvious tension between calling Jesus Lord and giving proper allegiance to Caesar; the missionary zeal of the church which threatened the polytheistic nature of the empire; suspicion arising from Christian practices (such as equating the Lord's Supper with cannibalism); and in the case of Nero, the need for scapegoats for the great fire in Rome in AD 64.

Of course, many groups in society are persecuted, and were persecuted in the first century. What is striking about the persecution of the early church is that there were no obvious benefits to its members in holding onto beliefs if they knew them to be false or had serious doubts about them. There was no social advantage to be gained from joining the church, as it did not initially carry the respectability which it was to attain later under Constantine. As the Archbishop of Canterbury said in his Easter sermon in 2006:

> It [the New Testament] was written by people who,
> by writing what they did and believing what they
> did, were making themselves, in the world's terms,
> less powerful, not more. They were walking out into
> an unmapped territory, away from the safe places of
> political and religious influence, away from traditional
> Jewish religion and from Roman society and law. As the
> Gospels and Paul's letters and the difficult, enigmatic
> letter "to the Hebrews" all agree, they were putting
> themselves in a place where they shared the humiliation
> experienced by condemned criminals going naked in
> public procession to their execution.[28]

While Christians in later generations, and adherents of other faiths, are prepared to suffer and even to die because of their belief in what they have been taught, the first Christians were in the position of being prepared to suffer and even to die because of their belief in what they had personally witnessed. It is difficult to argue convincingly that in these circumstances the first Christians did not genuinely believe, based on what they had seen and heard, that Jesus had been raised from the dead.

SUMMARY

- Something unexpected happened which led to the birth and explosive growth of the early church.

- This cannot be explained by any military or social factors, or by the continuing leadership of its "founder".

- The preaching, practices and response to persecution of the early church are consistent only with a central belief in the resurrection of Jesus.

CHAPTER 12

Evidence Outside
the New Testament

*In some circumstances it can be safely assumed that
if a certain event had occurred, evidence of it could
be discovered by qualified investigators. In such
circumstances it is perfectly reasonable to take the
absence of proof of its occurrence as positive proof of its
non-occurrence.*

Irving Copi (1953, 2010, page 95)

Court cases are decided on the basis of the evidence presented
to the court (together with consideration of the appropriate
principles of law). However, sometimes the absence of evidence
is also a factor. In a traffic accident claim brought by the
passenger of one car against the driver of another car, it would
be surprising if the driver of the first car did not give evidence
in support of the passenger, and the opponent would suggest
that this absence meant that the driver did not support the
passenger's claim. In a criminal prosecution, an alibi defence
that the accused was at home watching television with his
grandmother would be much weakened if the grandmother did
not give evidence supporting this.

Of course, there may be perfectly good reasons why the
evidence is not available. The witnesses may be abroad, unwell,
infirm, or may even have died. In each case it is necessary to
ask what evidence would be expected to be available. If it is

not available, any explanation for its absence will need to be considered. The absence of that evidence can then be weighed when considering the evidence that is actually before the court.

However, there are limits to the extent to which judges can make decisions based on the lack of evidence. In a case concerning the disappearance from storage of a painting by Rolf Harris, the judge was so concerned about the absence of the owner of the storage company, whom he described as "this missing *eminence grise*", that he reached the conclusion that the owner was personally and dishonestly responsible for its loss, even though this had not been alleged. In this case the Court of Appeal determined that the judge had gone too far (Hardy -v- Washington Green [2010] EWCA Civ 198).

Thus far, we have been considering principally evidence which derives from the New Testament and the early church. Most of what we know about Paul, James, and Peter comes from the New Testament documents. The accounts of the resurrection appearances which we have considered come primarily from the Gospels, supplemented by Paul's first letter to the Corinthians. Much of our information about the early church comes from Acts and the New Testament Epistles (letters), supplemented by the writings of early Christian "fathers". We now need to examine the evidence outside the New Testament, but before we do so, we need to ask what evidence we would expect to be available. In this respect, we should immediately note a number of considerations:

- As we have already seen, written information was not readily available in the first century. Unlike today's society, where copying is quick and easy, any document which needed copying in the first century had to be transcribed by hand onto papyrus, which was a time-consuming task. The cost of the materials was comparatively much greater than that of paper and ink today, and the whole procedure was very much less convenient than email or posting a blog online. Accordingly, very much less was committed to writing than is the case today. In short, we can expect only a tiny fraction of the written material we would expect to find about a person alive today.

- We have also noted that the events of Jesus' ministry took place in the relatively obscure Roman province of Palestine, and most of the events recorded before the last week of his life took place in Galilee rather than the major city of Jerusalem. The total length of his public ministry was about three years. We should therefore expect much less written material than we would if his ministry had spanned a long period in Jerusalem or Alexandria or Rome.

- Jesus had no official role, and therefore we should not expect any official record of his life or teachings. He did not lead a rebellion, so we should not expect any record as we would if there had been an uprising which had to be put down by the Romans. To put it bluntly, Jesus was not "famous" by the standards of his day, so there would be no reason for anyone to write about him. Any nascent, large-scale, popular support for him seemed to fade with his crucifixion.

- Relatively little written material survives from this period. This is partly because of the vulnerability of papyrus (being single sheets or scrolls), and partly because of the destruction and upheaval which resulted from the Jewish uprising in AD 66. Jerusalem was destroyed in AD 70, and the Jews were allowed only to retain a few sacred books. So, for example, the vast majority of the works of Nicolaus of Damascus, a close friend of Herod the Great, have been lost – only fragments remain of his 144-volume "universal history". Accordingly, unless there was a specific reason why writings were likely to be preserved (as would be the case with writings considered to be holy), there is a high possibility that they would be lost with the passage of time.

Pausing here, it will be clear that applying these general principles we can reasonably expect to find very little written material about Jesus outside the New Testament. But there is one further factor we need to consider:

- As is clear from our earlier consideration, the early church grew rapidly and over time began to produce writings, both records of Jesus' life and teachings and other documents referring to him. This includes the New Testament documents, but also the writings of early Christian "fathers" such as Clement, Ignatius, and Polycarp. However, anyone who is looking for independent evidence about the life of Jesus is likely to reject these sources as biased, on the basis that those who had committed their lives to the Christian faith are inherently likely to provide evidence corroborating the New Testament accounts. On the other hand, people outside the church would have no particular interest in writing about Jesus or the church unless it impacted upon them in some specific way. Therefore it is not realistic to expect vast amounts of independent written evidence about Jesus. In particular, it is very unlikely (as we shall see shortly) that anyone who was not a Christian would have written positively about the resurrection.

Given all these considerations, it might be supposed that there is no independent evidence at all about Jesus, but that is not so. In their book *The Case for the Resurrection of Jesus* Gary Habermas and Michael Licona identify forty-two separate authors who refer to Jesus within 150 years of his death. These include nine[29] authors of the New Testament (assuming that Paul, Peter and John wrote all the letters attributed to them – if they did not, the number would increase), twenty early Christian writers,[30] four writers of "heretical" Christian literature,[31] and nine secular writers.[32] If only the nine secular writers are considered, this accords precisely with the number of writers who refer to Tiberius (Roman Emperor at the time Jesus lived) within 150 years of his death. Luke also mentions Tiberius in Acts, but if we are to exclude him from one list then in fairness we should exclude him from both.

We can now turn to the significant references to Jesus by secular writers.

Josephus

Titus Flavius Josephus was a first-century Jewish and Roman historian. He had a colourful life, fighting for the Jews in the Jewish rebellion, captured and imprisoned by the Romans, and subsequently released and given Roman citizenship. He is the most prominent Jewish historian of the first century, writing a number of works including *The Wars of the Jews* and *Antiquities of the Jews*. He appears to refer to Jesus in two places. In *Antiquities* (20.9.1) he wrote:

> As therefore Ananus was of such a disposition, he
> thought he had now a good opportunity, as Festus was
> now dead, and Albinus was still on the road; so he
> assembled a council of judges, and brought it before the
> brother of Jesus the so-called Christ, whose name was

James, together with some others, and having accused
them as law-breakers, he delivered them over to be
stoned.

According to Louis Feldman, in "Josephus" in Volume 3 of the
Anchor Bible Dictionary, virtually all Josephus scholars accept
that this passage is genuine (pages 990–91). It is a passing
reference only, and the words "so-called Christ" are probably
used to distinguish Jesus from the other twenty people named
Jesus who appear in his writings. It is unlikely that Christian
editors seeking to add a reference to Jesus would have described
him as "the so-called Christ".

The same cannot be said for the second reference to Jesus
in Josephus' writings. This is far more controversial, and has
earned itself the title *testimonium Flavianum* ("witness of
Flavius"). In *Josephus and Modern Scholarship 1937–1980*
Feldman notes no less than eighty-seven distinct studies of this
passage. It is in the *Antiquities* (18.3.3). Here it is:

Now there was about this time Jesus, a wise man, if
it be lawful to call him a man. For he was a doer of
wonderful works, a teacher of such men as receive the
truth with pleasure. He drew over to him both many of
the Jews and many of the Gentiles. He was the Christ;
and when Pilate, at the suggestion of the principal men
among us, had condemned him to the cross, those that
loved him at the first ceased not, for he appeared to
them alive again the third day, as the divine prophets
had foretold these and ten thousand other wonderful
things concerning him; and the race of Christians, so
named from him, are not extinct even now.

As evidence from an apparently non-Christian writer, this is
simply too good to be true! A non-Christian, Jewish writer is

hardly likely to call Jesus "the Christ", or to say "if it is lawful to call him a man", or to say that Jesus appeared alive on the third day. Writing to Roman readers, he is unlikely to call Jesus "the Christ" (a peculiarly Jewish term), rather than "the so-called Christ" (used to identify this particular Jesus).

Thus it is likely that Christian editors have embellished what he originally wrote, although it has been pointed out that a Christian editor would have said that Jesus "*is* the Christ", not "*was* the Christ" (Thiede 2005, page 115). A few scholars consider the whole passage to be authentic, and a few consider the whole passage to be a forgery, but "the vast majority of scholars hold a middle position … claiming that Josephus wrote something about Jesus that was subsequently edited by Christian copyists" (Mason 2003, page 235). The problem then is to know what Josephus did write. A likely core attributable to Josephus would be as follows:

> Now there was about this time Jesus, a wise man. He
> was a doer of wonderful works, a teacher of such men
> as receive the truth with pleasure. He drew over to him
> both many of the Jews and many of the Gentiles; and
> when Pilate, at the suggestion of the principal men
> among us, had condemned him to the cross, those
> that loved him at the first ceased not; and the race of
> Christians, so named from him, are not extinct even
> now.

More might be added to this; for example an Arabic version is somewhat different, reading "they reported that he had appeared to them three days after his crucifixion and that he was alive; accordingly, he was perhaps the Messiah" which is much more likely than the traditional text. However, it is better that we proceed with caution and restrict the evidence to that which is most likely to be accurate.

Tacitus

Publius Cornelius Tacitus was a renowned Roman politician and historian who lived in the first and second centuries. His major works, the *Annals* and *Histories*, deal with the history of the Roman Empire in much of the first century (although substantial parts of these works have been lost). Writing in the *Annals* (15.44) about the great fire in Rome in AD 64, he said this:

> But all human efforts, all the lavish gifts of the emperor, and the propitiations of the gods, did not banish the sinister belief that the conflagration was the result of an order. Consequently, to get rid of the report, Nero fastened the guilt and inflicted the most exquisite tortures on a class hated for their abominations, called Christians by the populace. Christus, from whom the name had its origin, suffered the extreme penalty during the reign of Tiberius at the hands of one of our procurators, Pontius Pilate, and a deadly superstition, thus checked for the moment, again broke out not only in Judaea, the first source of the evil, but also in the City.

Similar information is given by another Roman historian of the same period Gaius Seutonius (many of whose works have also been lost), who wrote in *Lives of the Caesars* (16.2), "Punishment by Nero was inflicted on the Christians, a class of men given to a new and mischievous superstition."[33]

Pliny the Younger

Gaius Plinius Caecilius Secundus was a Roman lawyer and politician, whose surviving writings include the *Epistulae*, letters written by him. These include a letter written as Governor of Bithynia in Asia Minor to Emperor Trajan, asking how he should treat the Christians. In the letter (10.96–97) he writes:

> They were accustomed to meet on a fixed day before dawn and sing responsively a hymn to Christ as to a god, and bound themselves to a solemn oath, not to any wicked deeds, but never to commit any fraud, theft, adultery, never to falsify their word, not to deny a trust when they should be called upon to deliver it up. When this was over, it was their custom to depart and to assemble again to partake of a meal – but ordinary and innocent food.

Although these three Roman writers give important confirmation about the beliefs and persecution of the early church, they only take us a little way in relation to the life of Jesus. Tacitus confirms details of Jesus' death, and he and Seutonius refer to a "deadly superstition" and a "new and mischievous superstition". It is fascinating to speculate precisely what the new, mischievous and deadly superstition was – this clearly could be a reference to the belief in the resurrection, which was at the core of the belief and preaching of the early church.[34] Again, we cannot be certain, and as Tacitus was not alive at the time of Jesus' crucifixion, he must be relying on other sources which he does not specify.

The Talmud

The Talmud is a record of rabbinic discussions, and is made up of the Mishnah and the Gemara. It covers a wide range of subjects, and is believed to have been compiled between AD 200 and 500. It contains a number of passages that may refer to Jesus. Not surprisingly, they are all written in very negative terms, as the rabbis would undoubtedly have been hostile witnesses. It is not helpful to consider most of them, as they require a significant amount of explanation, for example as to why they are believed to refer to Jesus (as they do not use his name).[35] However, one (Babylonian Sanhedrin 43a) is of particular interest:

> On the eve of Passover they hanged Yeshu (of Nazareth) and the herald went before him for forty days saying (Yeshu of Nazareth) is going forth to be stoned in that he hath practiced sorcery and beguiled and led astray Israel. Let everyone knowing aught in his defence come and plead for him. But they found naught in his defence and hanged him on the eve of Passover.

The details do not accord with what we read in the Gospels and elsewhere, but this is confirmation from a hostile witness of Jesus' execution.

Therefore we have confirmation from non-Christian writers of the following facts:

- Jesus' existence (Josephus, Tacitus, Pliny, Talmud).

- Jesus performed "mighty works" (Josephus), or "sorcery" (Talmud).

- Jesus was "so-called" Christ (Josephus).

- Jesus had a brother named James (Josephus).

- Jesus was executed (Talmud) when Pilate was procurator (Josephus, Tacitus).

- Christians met on a fixed day and worshipped Jesus "as a god" (Pliny).

- Although there is no explicit reference to the resurrection, the references to a "deadly" and "new and mischievous" superstition may be references to the belief in the resurrection.

Early Christian writings

Although we have already noted that the writings of the early church cannot be seen as totally independent evidence, it is worthwhile mentioning those writings briefly, as they do consistently refer to the physical resurrection of Jesus. Examples from the first 150 years after Jesus' death include:

- Polycarp lived from AD 70 to 155, when he was martyred. He was a student of the apostle John. In Polycarp's Letter to the Philippians he refers several times (1:2; 2:1–2; 12:2) to God having raised Jesus from the dead.

- 1 Clement is a letter written to the church in Corinth by the church in Rome at the end of the first century. It contains a lengthy passage about resurrection, in which it states that God raised Jesus from the dead as "the first-fruits" (24:1).

- Ignatius was Bishop of Antioch in the late first and early second century, and was a disciple of the apostle John. He was also martyred. He wrote letters to a number of churches, which make several references to the resurrection. For example, he says in chapter 8 of his Letter to the Philadelphians, "My authentic archives are His cross, and death, and resurrection, and the faith which bears on these things."

- Aristides, a Greek Christian, produced an "apology" (a defence) which was either dedicated or delivered to Emperor Hadrian in the early second century. In explaining the basis of the Christian faith (which he contrasts with barbarian, Greek, and Jewish faith) he refers (in Section 2) to Jesus' resurrection after three days.

- Justin Martyr became a Christian in the middle of the second century, after studying under teachers of the Stoic, Aristotelian, Pythagorean, and Platonic philosophies. He wrote several documents, and made many references to Jesus' resurrection.[36]

SUMMARY

- Non-Christian writers in the first and early second centuries confirm a number of facts about Jesus' life and death, and the beliefs of the early church.
- There is no explicit reference by these writers to the resurrection.
- The earliest Christian writers refer consistently to Jesus' resurrection.

CHAPTER 13

The Gospels

Matthew, Mark, Luke, and John;
Acts and Romans follow on...

In the science-fiction comedy film *Galaxy Quest*, the crew of the NSEA *Protector* from a long-defunct television series (clearly based on *Star Trek*) are "recruited" by the peaceful alien race of Thermians, to help them face the evil warlord Sarris. The actors initially think they are appearing as actors, but soon realize that they have been transported into space, and the Thermians have built a working replica of the *Protector*. At the heart of the film is the fact that the Thermians have no concept of fiction, and have been receiving broadcasts of the *Galaxy Quest* series believing them to be "historical documents". They have no word for "actor" in their vocabulary, and the "captain" of the *Protector* is ultimately forced by Sarris to admit the truth to the Thermians, which he does by describing the actors using the only word which the Thermians will understand – "liars".

Christians through the ages have tended to accept without much questioning that the four Gospels are "historical documents". However, as we saw in an earlier chapter, there are a number of serious questions which need to be asked about the reliability of the Gospels, and any attempt to rely upon them as evidence for the resurrection without asking those questions is unlikely to satisfy anyone who does not already believe in the resurrection. Therefore this chapter will address some general questions about the Gospels, and the following chapter will look specifically at what they say about the resurrection.

Who wrote the Gospels?

As a general rule, evidence will be more reliable if we know who is giving it, and generally anonymous evidence is not admissible. None of the Gospels as we now have them identifies its author by name. However, Thiede suggests that details of the author would originally have been made public by means of a "sittybos", a parchment or leather strip attached to the handle of the scroll (Thiede 2005, page 105). It is certainly the case that from the second century the Gospels were generally accepted within the church as having been written by Matthew, Mark, Luke, and John.

The traditional view is that the author of Luke was the companion of Paul, who appears in the book of Acts, and who also wrote Acts (the author moves from third-person narrative to first-person narrative in Acts 16). Both books are dedicated to "Theophilus", and Acts commences, "In my former book, Theophilus, I wrote about all that Jesus began to do and to teach until the day he was taken up to heaven" (Acts 1:1–2). However, even if Luke was the author of the Gospel, he was not an apostle and he makes it clear that he was not himself an eyewitness to the events, as we have already noted (Luke 1:1–4).

The Gospel of Mark is said to have been written by John Mark, who is referred to in Acts 12:12 and elsewhere in Acts, and many believe him to be the young man "wearing nothing but a linen garment" referred to in Mark 14:51. Once again, John Mark was not an apostle, and the early Christian tradition is that his Gospel was based on the recollection of the apostle Peter. (Papias states that John the Elder said that "Mark became the interpreter of Peter".) However, this is not stated anywhere in the Gospel itself.

The author of the Gospel of John claims to be an eyewitness, or at least to be basing his writing on the evidence of an eyewitness – "the man who saw it has given testimony, and his testimony is true" (John 19:35), and the context suggests that this man was "the disciple whom [Jesus] loved" (John 19:26). Traditionally, this man is identified as John, son of Zebedee, who is specifically named in the other three Gospels but not in this one. Irenaeus identified the author as John, and he had been a pupil of Polycarp who in turn had been a pupil of John.

Of the four Gospels, the authorship of Matthew seems to be least certain. There is nothing in the Gospel itself which gives any indication of its author or whether the author was an eyewitness. There are a few second-century references to the author being the apostle Matthew, also known as Levi.

Whole volumes have been written dealing with the authorship of the four Gospels, and there is little point attempting even to summarize the arguments for and against here. It is fair to say that it is impossible to be certain that any one of the Gospels was actually written by the person whose name it bears in our modern-day versions of the New Testament. What can be said is that the written traditions as to authorship begin in the second century, only one or two generations after the Gospels were written. What can also be said with some certainty is that the authority of these four Gospels was accepted by the church at this early stage. In particular, Irenaeus (and there seems to be little doubt about who he was, or when he was writing!) said in *Against Heresies 3*:

> For as there are four quarters of the world in which
> we live, and four universal winds, and as the church is
> dispersed all over the earth, and the gospel is the pillar
> and base of the church and the breath of life, so it is
> natural that it should have four pillars. It is manifest
> that the Word, the architect of all things, who sits upon

the cherubim and holds all things together, having been manifested to men, has given us the gospel in fourfold form, but held together by one Spirit.

Professor F. F. Bruce (1955, 1984, page 109) comments on this passage that:

It is evident that by AD 180 the idea of the fourfold gospel had become so axiomatic throughout Christendom that it could be referred to as an established fact as obvious and inevitable and natural as the four cardinal points of the compass (as we call them) or the four winds.

When were the Gospels written?

This second question goes hand-in-hand with the first. If the Gospels were written by the "traditional" authors, then they must have been written in the middle to late first century, within the lifetime of Jesus' original followers. If, however, they were written by others, then they could have been written at a later stage. As a general rule, evidence will be more reliable the closer in time it is given to the events which it covers.

Over the centuries, there has been much debate as to the dating of the Gospels, and again the arguments in favour of earlier or later dating will not be rehearsed here. In the nineteenth century in particular, views were strongly expressed in favour of later (second-century) dates for the Gospels. However, more recent scholarship together with the discovery of more and earlier manuscripts and fragments has resulted in a very wide (if not totally unanimous) consensus that they were all written somewhere between AD 50 and 90.[37] In other words, they were written between twenty and sixty years after the events which they describe, and within the lifetime of Jesus' contemporaries.

Obviously, we would be much more satisfied with evidence produced within a much shorter period of the events themselves. However, as we have already noted, we must be careful here. We are living in an age of mass communication, where anything of importance (and much of no importance as well!) is recorded in writing within minutes. It would be wholly inappropriate to impose that standard on the first century, where very little was committed to writing. In those circumstances, there was a much stronger oral tradition, with people committing to memory important information in a way which now generally only happens in the few weeks running up to an exam.

Additionally we can observe that, even now, people do clearly recall significant events many years after they occurred. *The Times* on 11 May 2012 reported that Robert Jay QC, counsel to the Leveson Inquiry on Press Standards, had challenged Rupert Murdoch's claim not to remember a key lunch with Margaret Thatcher in 1981 (over thirty years earlier):

> One does at least have to question whether this is
> selective amnesia... the acquisition of the Times and
> its associated titles must have been one of the most
> important in his commercial life. This was a time
> of heightened emotion. Could an intimate lunch at
> Chequers really have been forgotten?

By pure coincidence, only a few days later a *Times* columnist commented on claims by Mitt Romney, the subsequent Republican candidate for US President, that he could not remember anything about bullying he was alleged to have been involved in when at school. The columnist questioned these claims, and stated that he could clearly remember an incident of bullying when he was at school. And many (including this author) can say the same.

Why were the Gospels written?

It is obvious that the Gospels were written by people who believed in Jesus, either for the benefit of others who already believed, or in an attempt to bring people to belief. Mark's Gospel commences, "The beginning of the good news about Jesus the Messiah, the Son of God" (Mark 1:1), and John's Gospel is stated to have been written "that you may believe [some manuscripts have 'continue to believe'] that Jesus is the Messiah, the Son of God, and that by believing you may have life in his name" (John 20:31). Furthermore, the writers also had specific purposes in writing as they did – the most obvious example is Matthew, which shows how Jesus fulfilled Old Testament prophecy. As a general rule, evidence is more reliable if it has not been produced for an "ulterior" purpose.

The first question we must ask is whether the Gospels are "history" in any of the senses which we have considered. They are certainly not biographies of the type we are accustomed to read today. A modern biography would set out in considerable detail the family background of the subject, focusing in particular on the subject's parents. Apart from the genealogies in Matthew and Luke, the Gospels tell us nothing about Jesus' family background and very little indeed about his parents, Mary and Joseph. A modern biography would consider the subject's childhood, education, and adolescence. Mark and John say nothing at all about Jesus' upbringing. Matthew narrates his birth, but says nothing more. Luke also deals with his birth and with a single incident when he was twelve, and then comments that "Jesus grew in wisdom and stature, and in favour with God and man" (Luke 2:41–52). With that exception, the Gospels tell us nothing about Jesus' life between his birth and the beginning of his public ministry, which is generally thought to have begun when he was aged around thirty.

So were there other biographies of this type being written in the first century AD? In his book *The New Testament Gospels* C. F. Evans asks (page 7) how a librarian at the famous library in Alexandria would have classified Mark's Gospel. He suggests that it would not easily fit within any of the general categories of writing at the time, whether "lives of famous men" (focusing on the most significant events in the subject's life, as a means of illuminating their character), "acts" (narrating the heroic deeds of a famous person) or "memoirs" (a collection of anecdotes about and sayings of a famous person). Although the Gospels have similarities to all of these categories, they are also different from them. In short, they represent a new genre of writing.

The word "gospel" itself means "good news", and the Greek word was not used for a literary genre, but referred to the equivalent of a celebratory headline – good news of a victory or the accession of a new emperor. Having said this, the Gospel writers themselves did not use the term "gospel" to describe what they had written – Mark's use of the word refers to the good news about Jesus, not to the fact that he was writing "a gospel". The use of the word "gospel" in the New Testament is always in the context of the speaking or preaching of the good news about Jesus, and Matthew, Mark, Luke, and John only acquired the description of "Gospels" some time in the second century.

Ralph Martin (1975, page 43) suggests that the Gospels are historical, but are "history with a novel twist". They did not follow any existing literary convention, but "are theological documents which set out the interpreted history of the person Jesus of Nazareth... In the phrase 'interpreted history', both aspects are to be given equal prominence."

Put simply, the writers of the Gospels were not concerned only to record facts about Jesus or teachings by him. Rather, they chose which facts and teachings to include and exclude based on their theological objectives. Indeed, the writer of John's Gospel expressly states that "Jesus performed many other signs in the presence of his disciples, which are not recorded in this book" (John 20:30).[38]

Does this mean that we should automatically assume that the Gospels are unreliable as sources of information about Jesus? That is certainly the view taken by some, particularly members of the "Jesus Seminar" who have voted on the likely authenticity of much of the Gospels, and have concluded that much of the material cannot be relied upon. The presuppositions and methods used by the Seminar have been extensively criticized, for example their rejection of the sayings of Jesus which are too similar to the beliefs of Judaism or the early church. (Given that Jesus had a Jewish background, and that the church initially comprised Jesus' close followers, it would be astonishing if Jesus' sayings were *not* similar to the beliefs of Judaism, and if the teachings of the early church were *not* similar to Jesus' sayings).[39]

It is more illuminating to consider the approach of an expert in literature from the same period as the Gospels. A. N. Sherwin-White, whom we shall consider in more detail in a later chapter, accepted that the Gospels were in one sense a "propaganda narrative", but rejected the conclusion that this meant that they were unreliable. He made a comparison with the work of Herodotus (who is generally known as "the father of history"), whose writings were also "the vehicle of a moral or a religious idea which shapes the narrative", but stated that this "presents no intractable difficulty to a critical historian" (1963, page 190).

So we must recognize the Gospels for what they are – history written for a theological purpose. We may need to treat them with caution as a consequence, but not with any more caution than other literature of the same period. If they were, as seems reasonable to believe, written within the lifetime of Jesus' contemporaries, it is simply not realistic to think that they could have been largely fictitious and still accepted as authoritative and reliable by the early church.

How were the Gospels chosen?

This brings us neatly to the fourth question. It is suggested in *The Da Vinci Code* that the four Gospels that we have in the New Testament were selected from many more in the fourth century. In particular, they were preferred to gospels which stressed Jesus' human traits. It is worth noting that even the basis of this suggestion is wrong – the four Gospels show a very human Jesus – a Jesus who ate and drank, got tired and slept, who became angry and wept. However, it is true that numerous other gospels were written, and that only four were chosen for inclusion in the New Testament.

Once again, whole books have been written about this (see for example Hill 2010), and a detailed consideration of the issues cannot be undertaken here. In very simple terms, the evidence from the writings of the early church fathers is that the four Gospels in the New Testament were accepted by the early church as being the only authoritative gospels at a very early stage in the second century. Not only is the fourfold tradition referred to expressly (see Irenaeus' comments earlier in this chapter) but the contents of the Gospels are quoted extensively. Indeed, it has been said by scholars that if the New Testament had not existed as such, we would have almost the entire content of the New Testament available in the writings of the early Christians.[40] The writings of Ignatius, writing about AD 108 and Polycarp, writing about AD 110, confirm that the Gospels were in circulation by that time, and Clement, writing about AD 96, refers to Matthew, Mark, and Luke.

Many other gospels were written, but it is generally accepted that most of them were written at a much later date. Certainly none of them ever gained widespread acceptance in the early church. That is categorized by some as evidence of a conspiracy, but the much simpler explanation is that the early church did not accept that those gospels accurately reflected what they believed about Jesus, and those beliefs included what they believed about his life, death, and resurrection. While the concept of revisionist history is well known – the critical re-examination of presumed facts and their interpretation – the other (apocryphal) gospels present a sometimes very different picture of the life of Jesus, without any attempt critically to examine the earlier material. In some cases, as we shall see, the account which each one presents is, in the literal sense of the word, unbelievable.

Bruce Metzger neatly summarizes the reason for "choosing" the four Gospels for inclusion in the New Testament as follows: "the canon [the approved list of New Testament books] is a list of authoritative books more than it is an authoritative list of books" (quoted in Strobel 1998, page 69). In other words, when the New Testament was put together, the early church did not "choose", and thereby confer authority on the four Gospels, but it recognized their existing authority. One might say that, in this way, the Gospels "chose" themselves. Francis Spufford, at the end of a highly entertaining passage on the choice of the four Gospels, comments: "Read much of the rival 'gospels', and you start to think that the Church Fathers who decided what went into the New Testament had one of the easiest editorial jobs on record" (2012, page 156).

Do the Gospels contain contradictions?

There is one final issue to be addressed, and that is the apparent contradictions between the four Gospels. We will need to look at this in some detail when we move on to consider the Gospel accounts of the resurrection, but it is worth considering the issue generally here. In doing so, we must recall the need to identify our prejudices. For many Christians, the suggestion that there may be contradictions and inconsistencies is unthinkable, and accordingly they will not even contemplate the idea. To even raise the issue will suggest to them a lack of faith, and any whiff of contradiction is "apparent" rather than real. On the other hand, there are those who dispute entirely the historic value of the Gospels, and who therefore seize upon any apparent contradiction as vindication of their view, without asking whether there might be a reasonable explanation. Neither approach is of any help in attempting an open-minded consideration of the evidence.

Readers will by now be weary of the refrain that "whole books have been written on the topic", but this is particularly so here! It is undeniable that there are apparent contradictions between the Gospels. We will consider here just one well-known example – the healing of the blind man Bartimaeus.

The story is told in three of the Gospels (Matthew 20:29–34; Mark 10:46–52; Luke 18:35–43). In Mark, one blind man was healed as Jesus was leaving Jericho. In Matthew, two blind men were healed as Jesus was leaving Jericho. In Luke, one blind man was healed as Jesus was approaching Jericho. To explain the "apparent" contradictions, various suggestions have been made. It is possible (although exceptionally unlikely as these deal with the same point in time in Jesus' ministry) that there were two or three separate occasions of healing. If there was only one, then we may harmonize in these ways: Mark and Luke may have been focusing in particular upon Bartimaeus, but that is not inconsistent with there having been two men healed; and Jesus may have been both leaving (the old city of) and approaching (the new city) of Jericho, as a new city had been built by Herod to the south of the old city, which was largely abandoned.

Such explanations are likely to satisfy those eager to accept the literal truth of all three accounts, and to be entirely unsatisfactory to those who do not accept their literal truth.

A more open-minded approach is to accept that the details recorded are different, but the fundamental basis of the story is unchanged. In all three accounts, one blind man is healed by Jesus on the outskirts of Jericho. It is irrelevant to the fundamental basis of the story whether there was a second blind man and which way Jesus was heading when he met the man. It is a hallmark of honestly given evidence that the details will differ. People generally do not have photographic memories, and their testimony will usually differ on issues such as precise times, specific words used, perception of speed and distance, and so on. Indeed, suspicions tend to be roused not by witnesses who differ in relation to detail, but by those who give accounts which are word-for-word identical. What the court looks for is the underlying basis of the evidence.

This approach can usefully be adopted in relation to all the apparent contradictions in the Gospels. The question should be asked, what is the underlying story being told? If that can be identified, then differences in the detail can be accepted for what they are – differences in recollection based on the fact that the Gospels were compiled from various sources (whether four entirely independent eyewitnesses, four compilations of the evidence of others, or some other combination). Christians who treasure every word of the Bible need not feel threatened by this approach, because all Scripture is said to be "God-breathed" and "useful" (2 Timothy 3:16). There is no reason why it cannot be useful even if the details of parallel accounts are different.

SUMMARY

- The four New Testament Gospels were a new genre of writing.

- A number of challenges have been raised to the historical reliability of the Gospels, each of which can be answered.

- At the very least, the Gospels can be relied upon to corroborate other evidence. At the very best, they comprise four independent eyewitness accounts.

CHAPTER 14

The Gospels' Resurrection Accounts

For any half competent cross-examiner, dealing with the post-resurrection accounts is like shooting rats in a barrel.

The final issue which we considered in the last chapter was that of inconsistencies between the Gospels. This is particularly acute for the basic subject matter of this book – the resurrection of Jesus. The words at the top of this page are put into the mouth of a fictional character presenting the non-Christian view in a debate by one author, a barrister.[41] A superficial consideration of the four Gospel accounts would seem to support this view, as set out in the following table:

Event	Matthew	Mark	Luke	John
Rolling away the stone	Violent earthquake; an angel rolled the stone away	Not mentioned	Not mentioned	Not mentioned
Women at the tomb	Mary Magdalene and "the other Mary"	Mary Magdalene, Salome, and Mary the mother of James	Mary Magdalene, Joanna, Mary the mother of James, and others	Mary Magdalene

Was The Tomb Empty?

Event	Matthew	Mark	Luke	John
Whom the women met	An angel	A young man in white	Two men in clothes that gleamed like lightning	See "Mary Magdalene" below
The women's response	They ran to tell the disciples and met Jesus on the way	They were afraid and said nothing	They told the disciples, who did not believe	See "Mary Magdalene" below
Mary Magdalene	See above	Jesus appeared first to her; she told the others who did not believe	See above	Mary told Simon and John about the empty tomb, then met two angels, and then met Jesus
Peter	Not mentioned	Not mentioned	Peter saw the linen strips in the tomb	Peter and John saw the linen strips in the tomb
Emmaus Road	Not mentioned	Jesus appeared "in a different form" to two walking in the country	Jesus appeared to Cleopas and another on the way to Emmaus, and was revealed as Jesus in the breaking of bread	Not mentioned
Appearance to the eleven disciples	Not mentioned	Jesus appeared to them while they were eating and rebuked them	Jesus appeared to them and ate	Jesus appeared to them in the absence of Thomas, and for a second time a week later when Thomas was there

Event	Matthew	Mark	Luke	John
Miraculous catch of fish and reinstatement of Peter	Not mentioned	Not mentioned	Not mentioned	Last recorded appearance
Great commission/ ascension	At a mountain in Galilee	Follows on from the appearance to the eleven	At Bethany	Not mentioned

What are we to make of all this?

As a preliminary point, we should note that the earliest manuscripts of Mark's Gospel do not contain verses 9 to 20 of chapter 16. The earliest manuscripts end at verse 8: "Trembling and bewildered, the women went out and fled from the tomb. They said nothing to anyone, because they were afraid." There has been considerable scholarly debate about this. One view is that this was the original ending, a sort of "whodunit" (or, more accurately, a "whatwasdun") inviting the reader to reach his or her own conclusion about the empty tomb. This seems highly unlikely, not least because of the emphasis in the rest of the Gospel upon the predictions by Jesus of his suffering, death and resurrection – it would be very surprising if Mark intended to write about the fulfilment of the first two elements and not the third, and this would hardly be the good news proclaimed in his opening words. (See Appendix 5 for a summary of reasons why I do not consider 16:8 to be the original ending, and see N. T. Wright, 2003, pages 617–24, for a much fuller exploration of the issue.)

A second view is that verses 9 to 20 are the original ending. This also seems unlikely. The style of the verses is very different from what has come before, even to those who cannot read the original Greek. Mark's Gospel is full of detailed narrative, but these verses seem to contain brief summaries of the resurrection appearances, in the style of someone who has run out of time in an exam, and is finishing off quickly with a list of bullet points.

The final view is that the original ending was lost (or that Mark was unable to complete it), and that verses 9 to 20 were added by another writer to bring the Gospel to an appropriate conclusion. This is feasible, as the ends of a scroll (upon which the Gospel would have been written) would be far more vulnerable than the rest of it. If this is what did happen, we can only speculate as to what the original ending would have said.

There are several points which need to be made in seeking to assess how much weight we should place on the evidence of the Gospel accounts.

It may be possible to harmonize the accounts

Although the accounts appear at first to be hopelessly inconsistent, a much more careful and thorough analysis may resolve some if not all of the problems. Many attempts have been made to do this, and Appendix 4 contains a summary of one of the most compelling.

The accounts are not intended to be comprehensive

It is essential to remember that the Gospel accounts are not intended to be four complete accounts of the same events. We have already seen how John states this expressly as a general point, and Luke tells us in Acts that Jesus "gave many convincing proofs that he was alive" and "appeared to them over a period of forty days" (Acts 1:3), even though this is not apparent from his Gospel. The detail of the resurrection appearances reinforces this. For example:

- In Luke 24:34 the disciples say that "The Lord has risen and has appeared to Simon." There is no record in Luke, or in any other Gospel, of that appearance to Simon Peter. However, we may recall that such an appearance is mentioned by Paul in 1 Corinthians. Not only do Luke and 1 Corinthians corroborate each other, but it is clear that Luke is aware of, but has chosen not to give details of, Jesus' appearance to Simon Peter.

- In Luke 24:24 the two disciples on the Emmaus road tell Jesus that "some of our companions went to the tomb and found it just as the women had said". However, in Luke 24:12 only Peter is recorded as going to the tomb. So the fact that only one person is mentioned does not mean that others were not involved.

- Likewise, in John 20:2 Mary Magdalene says to Simon Peter and the one identified as the "beloved disciple" that "they have taken the Lord out of the tomb, and we don't know where they have put him!" Verse 1 only mentions Mary going to the tomb, but as she uses the word "we" it implies that there were others there whom John has not mentioned.

- In Mark 16:7 (so in the undisputed part of Mark) the young man says to the women, "But go, tell his disciples and Peter, 'He is going ahead of you into Galilee. There you will see him, just as he told you.'" There is no mention in the rest of the Gospel of anything happening in Galilee. However, both Matthew and John do narrate meetings between Jesus and the disciples in Galilee. So Mark corroborates Matthew and John.

Once we realize that the Gospel writers were not intending to include all of the resurrection appearances, or all of the details of a particular appearance, many of the apparent contradictions fall away, or at least reduce dramatically. For example the conundrum of one or two men or angels. The fact that only one is mentioned in two of the Gospels is not inconsistent with the other Gospels mentioning two. And angels are described in places in the Old Testament as appearing in human form, so there is no necessary inconsistency between the two – in Genesis 19 the "angels" of verse 1 and 15 are also described as "men" in verses 5, 10, 12 and 16.

Wenham (1984, page 52) suggests that the Gospel writers are "not attempting a leisurely account of the whole history. They are more like advocates in a court of law, with limited time and space, trying to summon the most telling evidence."

The accounts do not describe the resurrection itself

If the writers of the Gospels were setting out to create a fictional account of the resurrection, it is highly likely that they would have included an account of the resurrection itself. Indeed, that is precisely what we see in the Gospel of Peter (9:34 – 10:42), which most commentators believe to have been written in the second century. Part of this reads:

> They saw again three men come out from the sepulchre, and two of them sustaining the other, and a cross following them, and the heads of the two reaching to heaven, but that of him who was led of them by the hand overpassing the heavens. And they heard a voice out of the heavens crying, "Hast thou preached to them that sleep?" and from the cross there was heard the answer, "Yea."

This account, with its moving, talking cross, is both spectacular and spectacularly unbelievable. With the exception of Matthew's account of an earthquake, an angel rolling away the stone from the entrance to the tomb and the dead being raised from their tombs (Matthew 28:2; 27:53), there is nothing remotely spectacular about the accounts in the four Gospels, and indeed the reader is struck by the sheer ordinariness of much of what happens: Jesus being mistaken for a gardener; Jesus walking, talking and eating; the disciples being afraid and confused. There is quite simply no attempt to describe the process (if that is even the right word) of the resurrection itself.

The accounts are strange

This may seem to be a peculiar argument in support of the accuracy of the Gospel accounts, but the only way to describe the risen Jesus after reading the accounts is "strange". In some respects he has a physical body – he walks and talks, eats and drinks, touches and is touched. In other respects he is quite unlike a physical person – he appears and disappears. On some occasions he is instantly recognizable; on others he is not. N. T. Wright (2003, page 477) proposes the use of a new word, "transphysical", to describe Jesus' body, to reflect the fact that it is still physical but that it has been transformed.

It is telling that the Gospel writers make no attempt to resolve the strangeness, as we would expect them to do if they were seeking to create an account purely so that it would be believed, rather than reporting what had actually occurred. Additionally, as Wright points out, there were Old Testament passages which were available to them if they had been seeking a description of a resurrected body, particularly Daniel 12:3 which refers to the wise rising to "shine like the brightness of the heavens … like the stars for ever and ever". Matthew, Mark, and Luke all record Jesus being transfigured *before* his death: "His clothes became dazzling white, whiter than anyone in the world could bleach them" (Mark 9:3). Why, then, did they not adopt this type of language to describe him after his resurrection, instead of presenting such a strange picture? The obvious answer is that they were reporting what the witnesses had actually experienced, rather than what people might have expected.

The role of the women

As we have seen, all four Gospels record that the first people to find the tomb empty were women, and only women saw the men/angels. Two of the Gospels also record that the first appearance of Jesus was to women. This may not seem surprising to us, but it would have been nothing short of astonishing in first-century Palestine. There is some dispute as to whether women could give evidence under any circumstances at all – Josephus said, "From women let no evidence be accepted, because of the levity and temerity of their sex" (*Antiquities* 4.219), although John Wenham (1984, page 150, note 26) notes that female witnesses were acceptable as to matters within their own knowledge if there were no male witnesses available. At the very least, therefore, we can say that in first-century Judaism the testimony of a woman was significantly inferior to that of a man.

The importance given to the female witnesses in the Gospels is highly noteworthy. If the authors had been seeking to produce an account which was likely to be believed, it would have been much more logical for them to have chosen male witnesses. There were many candidates available – not only Jesus' close disciples but also his other followers, including Joseph of Arimathea and Nicodemus, members of the Sanhedrin who had been responsible for burying Jesus (all four gospels identify Joseph. John refers also to Nicodemus). Once again, it is difficult to explain why the

Gospel writers did this unless they were recording what actually happened, rather than writing polished fiction.

Inconsistencies

Even if attempts to harmonize the Gospel accounts so as to remove all inconsistencies are unsuccessful, this does not mean that the accounts should simply be disregarded. The historian A. N. Sherwin-White (1963, page 187) makes this point by reference to the sources for our knowledge of Tiberius Caesar, a contemporary of Jesus, saying that it is still possible to write a history of Tiberius' life despite the discrepancies. And courts deal daily with evidence which contains inconsistencies.

Indeed, as we have already noted, it may not be going too far to say that the presence of some inconsistencies between the accounts given by witnesses is a sign that their evidence may be true. Judges and juries are extremely sceptical about witnesses whose accounts agree exactly, particularly when they relate to events which were unplanned and unexpected. People's recollections differ, particularly in the heat of the moment, and so evidence which is identical strongly suggests that there has been collusion between the witnesses, or at the very least some impermissible "coaching" of the witnesses by their lawyers.

I have some personal experience of this, not only from two and a half decades dealing with evidence on a professional basis, but also from giving evidence myself. One evening I was sitting in my parents' dining room when I saw someone come into the garden, approach the house, and then bend down. I went out to see what was happening, and a young man was leaving the garden carrying a brick which he had obviously picked up. Outside, a middle-aged man was arguing with a group of young men. The man with the brick joined in the argument, and then threw the brick at the older man from a distance of about four feet, causing a messy head injury. The young men scattered. In due course, a young man was arrested and charged with assault. I gave evidence at the trial, as did the older man, and a woman who had been with him, a woman who had also seen the altercation out of her first floor window on the other side of the road. The evidence of the four of us in our witness statements and in court differed in many respects – how many young men there had been, their height and the clothing they wore, precisely who said what to whom. However, it agreed about the essentials – that that particular young man had thrown the brick. He was duly convicted.

So it is with the Gospels. There is no attempt to produce accounts without inconsistencies; indeed we have seen that there are loose ends within the individual accounts themselves even before we begin to compare them with one another. But they agree on the essential points – Jesus was crucified, died, and was buried; the tomb was found to be empty and the disciples experienced the risen Jesus. Beyond those essentials, many of the details do agree between the Gospels, particularly when we bear in mind the points made earlier in this chapter. As we have observed more than once, this is an indication that the Gospel writers are seeking to record the evidence of the witnesses, rather than trying to produce a watertight or air-brushed version.

SUMMARY

- At first, the four Gospel accounts of the resurrection seem so inconsistent as to be unbelievable.

- However, on closer examination, there are many points which suggest that they are essentially accurate accounts of the witnesses.

- At the very least, the accounts can be relied upon to corroborate other evidence. At the very best, they comprise four independent eyewitness accounts.

CHAPTER 15

Expert Evidence

We do not have trial by expert in this country; we have
trial by judge.

Stuart-Smith LJ

(Liddell -v- Middleton [1996] PIQR page 43)

As we have seen, the judge's first task is to reach a decision in relation to disputed facts; having done this, he will apply the law to those facts. So in a road traffic accident claim, the judge will first decide what happened and will then decide who is legally responsible based on that first decision.

We have also seen that the decision in relation to the disputed facts must be made applying the burden and standard of proof to the evidence which is put before the judge. That evidence will principally relate to what the witnesses saw, heard, or otherwise perceived using their senses. As a general principle, the opinions and beliefs of witnesses are not admissible to prove disputed facts. This is principally because it is the function of the judge or jury, not the witness, to reach a conclusion about the facts.

To give a simple example, if a witness says, "The car was being driven too fast for the road conditions," this will be an opinion which is not admissible, as it is for the judge or jury to reach a decision on that issue. On the other hand, if the witness says, "It was a thirty-miles-per-hour speed limit. As the car overtook me, I looked at my speedometer and saw that I was driving at thirty," this will be admissible evidence of what the witness actually saw.

One exception to the general principle excluding opinion evidence is that which is given by experts. The rationale for this is that experts have a particular skill or training which enables them to form opinions based on facts. The dividing line between expert evidence which is or is not admissible is still uncertain in some cases. There is no doubt that medical experts can give evidence about the extent to which a person's injuries were caused by an accident. There is equally little doubt that the evidence of accident reconstruction experts is not normally permitted, because it is for the judge or jury to decide what happened (an exception might be where the available evidence is limited because a party has been killed in the accident or cannot remember what happened). It is less clear to what extent engineers should be permitted to give evidence about whether the damage to the vehicles is consistent with the alleged accident and the injury alleged to have been suffered.

Obviously it is essential that the experts have the necessary skill, training, and experience to give a reliable opinion in relation to a particular issue. It is also essential that they are independent of the parties, so that the court can be satisfied that they are providing impartial evidence. To facilitate this, there are rules that set out the duties of experts providing evidence in court.

Applying these principles to the issue of Jesus' resurrection, we can immediately see the limits to which expert evidence can assist. The ultimate question of whether Jesus did rise from the dead is one which has to be decided on the basis of the evidence, and the opinions of experts about this, while they may be interesting, would not be admissible evidence (quite apart from the problem of finding anyone with the appropriate skill, training, and experience to give such an opinion!)

However, there are other issues relating to the evidence itself in respect of which experts may be able to provide an opinion. Indeed, some opinion evidence has already been mentioned, even though it was not specifically identified at that point (for example, the statement in Chapter 13 by Bruce Metzger on the selection of the Gospels). It must immediately be recognized that these experts will not be completely independent, in that they may or may not already have a belief in the resurrection, and this may (consciously or subconsciously) affect their opinion. For this reason, we will exclude experts whose field is restricted to biblical studies in some way, including theologians and Bible translators. We will focus on experts who had a significant reputation in a particular area which is relevant to the issue we are considering.

Palaeography

This is the study of ancient manuscripts. Sir Frederic Kenyon GBE, KCB, TD was Director and Principal Librarian of the British Museum for twenty-one years, and also held other positions including President of the British Academy and of the Hellenic Society. His obituary in *The Times* (25 August 1952) stated that "it is doubtful whether the museum has ever had or will have a director more variously distinguished or with so striking a combination of qualities". While at the British Museum, he was involved in the consideration of biblical manuscripts, and after his retirement was involved in the acquisition and publication of two extremely important New Testament manuscripts, the Codex Sinaiticus[42] and the Chester Beatty papyri.[43]

Kenyon wrote numerous books, a number of which dealt with the Bible and its source texts. In 1940 he wrote *The Bible and Archaeology*, in which he considered the principal results of archaeological research in relation to the Bible. He acknowledged (page 8) that he was not primarily an archaeologist, and to that extent he relied upon the work of others. He made it clear that he did not believe in an infallible Bible (page 26), but suggested that we should use the faculties given to us by God to study the biblical documents (page 21). Having considered the nature of archaeological evidence generally, and then in some detail the different types of archaeological evidence available, and from different areas of the Middle East, he concluded by considering the total results of the evidence on our understanding of the Old and New Testament respectively. In relation to the New Testament, this evidence was almost exclusively in the form of manuscripts, which fell within his area of expertise and experience, and he concluded (page 289):

> The interval between the dates of original composition and the earliest extant evidence becomes so small as to be in fact negligible, and the last foundation for any doubt that the scriptures have come down to us substantially as they were written has now been removed. Both the *authenticity* and the *general integrity* of the books of the New Testament may be regarded as finally established.

As always, it is important to read the expert's evidence in context, for Kenyon goes on to say that this conclusion does not mean that we can be certain as to all the details of the New Testament records. He then summarizes the progress made in textual criticism as different manuscripts with variant readings have been considered, and makes this assertion (page 300):

> In the existence of various readings, therefore, there is nothing strange or disquieting. On the contrary, it is satisfactory to find that, in spite of all these varieties of detail, the substance of the record remains intact.

Ancient history

Adrian Sherwin-White was a tutor at St John's College Oxford from 1936 and a Reader in Ancient History at Oxford University from 1966 to 1979. He specialized in Roman history and gained an international reputation for his prize-winning exposition on Roman citizenship published in 1939, which became the standard work on the subject. He also published works on racial prejudice in imperial Rome, Roman foreign policy and the letters of Pliny. (His obituary in *The Times*, 15 November 1993, contains fuller details.)

In 1960–61 Sherwin-White gave the Sarum Lectures, which were published by Oxford University Press in 1963 under the title *Roman Society and Roman Law in the New Testament*. The dust jacket of the 1965 edition states:

> this book deals with Roman Public Law, Municipal Law and Usage in the Gospels and Acts of the Apostles. Its aim is to put New Testament scholars and historically minded Bible readers in touch with the more recent developments of Roman historical research, which have not been fully appreciated in some recent Biblical studies.

Sherwin-White considered specifically the trials of Jesus and Paul, in the light of Roman law and the legal system at the time. In general terms he concluded that the accounts accorded with what is otherwise known of the Roman legal system at the time – for example, "The account of the trial before Festus and Felix is then sufficiently accurate in all its details" (page 68) and, "As documents these narratives belong to the same historical series as the record of provincial and imperial trials in epigraphical and literary sources in the first and early second centuries AD" (page 121).

He went on to consider the social background to the Gospels in Galilee. As with Kenyon, he clearly did not believe that the Gospels were infallible, but he concluded (page 138):

> When one lays aside the Graeco-Roman spy-glass and looks at the narrative in another manner, it coheres beautifully. The pattern of life, both social and economic, civil and religious, is precisely what is to be expected in the isolated district of Galilee, a land which retained its Jewish characteristics long after the christianisation of Judaea. The absence of Graeco-Roman colouring is a convincing feature of the Galilean narrative and parables. Rightly, it is only when the scene changes to Jerusalem that the Roman administrative machine manifests itself…

Having considered questions of Roman citizenship, Sherwin-White dealt finally with "the question of historicity". He pointed out that in general terms, a "hard core or basic layer of historical truth" can be determined even from very poor sources, because of the existence of external corroborating evidence and the "synoptic principle" (a basic unitary tradition underneath the differences of detail in different sources). He contrasted the records of Jesus' life with those of his contemporary Tiberius Caesar, which "disagree amongst themselves in the wildest possible fashion" (page 187) but which do not preclude the construction of a history of his life. Because of the Greco-Roman setting of Acts, "the confirmation of historicity is overwhelming … any attempt to reject its historicity even in matters of detail must now appear absurd. Roman historians have long taken it for granted" (page 189). He rejected the idea that the Gospels represented "didactic myths" because of the timescale involved and, as we have seen, drew a parallel with the works of Herodotus (page 190). This demonstrated that even allowing two generations between the events and the record of them would not enable the mythical tendency to prevail over the hard core of history. He considered that the impression of a historical tradition was particularly felt in the accounts of Jesus' trial, which he had already considered at some length.

Literature

In addition to his well-known *Narnia Chronicles* C. S. Lewis wrote science fiction and a number of popular books that considered different aspects of the Christian faith. He was certainly an extremely overt Christian, but he was also highly regarded in his field of literature – a recent book review described him as "a shrewd literary critic and brilliant lecturer".[44] He was a Fellow and Tutor at Magdalen College Oxford from 1924 to 1954, Professor of Medieval and Renaissance English at Cambridge from 1954 to 1963, and a Fellow of the British Academy. His book *The Allegory of Love* won the Hawthornden Prize.

We have already encountered Lewis' views on the possibility that the Gospels are legends. As a literary historian, Lewis rejected that suggestion: "I have read a great deal of legend and I am quite clear that they are not the same sort of thing. They are not artistic enough to be legends."[45] He therefore concluded that the resurrection accounts were not legends – if they were not what they purported to be, they were either lunacy or lies! He returned to this theme in a talk given to students at Westcott House, a theological college at Cambridge. This was subsequently published under the title "Modern Theology and Biblical Criticism", and was later republished with the rather more intriguing title *Fern-Seed and Elephants*. He was speaking in response to the works of New Testament critics who denied the historicity of the Gospels, and said this (page 106):

whatever these men may be as Biblical critics, I distrust them as critics. They seem to me to lack literary judgment, to be imperceptive about the very quality of the texts they are reading… If he tells me that something in a Gospel is legend or romance, I want to know how many legends and romances he has read, how well his palate is trained in detecting them by the flavour; not how many years he has spent on that Gospel.

He went on to give the example of a scholar who had described John's Gospel as a "spiritual romance" and "a poem not a history", and said (page 108):

I have been reading poems, romances, vision-literature, legends, myths all my life. I know what they are like. I know that not one of them is like this. Of this text there are only two possible views. Either this is reportage – though it no doubt contains errors – pretty close up to the facts; nearly as close as Boswell. Or else, some unknown writer in the second century, without known predecessors or successors, suddenly anticipated the whole technique of modern, novelistic, realistic narrative. If it is untrue, it must be narrative of that kind. The reader who doesn't see this has simply not learned to read.

On this point, he concluded that such scholars "claim to see fern-seed and can't see an elephant ten yards away in broad daylight" (page 111).

Law

When it comes to giving expert evidence, lawyers have little part to play. This is because it is for the judge to form an opinion on any disputed issue of law or fact, assisted by submissions from any lawyers instructed in the case. It is only very rarely that lawyers are permitted to give expert evidence – it may for example be necessary where the judge has to decide issues relating to a foreign law. So the views of lawyers carry relatively little weight as we consider the evidence about the resurrection. They are in the same position as you, although with the advantage of having considerable experience of weighing evidence. We shall merely note that eminent lawyers throughout the years have examined the evidence and have been convinced by it.

In the mid-nineteenth century Professor Simon Greenleaf, the author of the leading US text on the law of evidence, wrote a book entitled *An Examination of the Testimony of the Four Evangelists, by the Rules of Evidence Administered in Courts of Justice.* He concluded that, by applying the rules of evidence, the testimony of the Gospel writers should be admitted to be true unless they could be disproved, but even if the burden of proof was reversed, it was still "capable of a ready moral demonstration" based on their honesty, their ability, their number and consistency of testimony, the conformity of their testimony with experience, and the coincidence of their testimony with collateral circumstances.[46]

More recently British academic lawyers have reached the conclusion that the evidence is reliable (notably Professor Sir Norman Anderson QC 1969; Professor John Warwick Montgomery 1986) and Christian judges have included Lord Chancellors Hailsham of St Marylebone (1970–1974 and 1979–1987) and Mackay of Clashfern (1987–1997) and probably the best-known judge of the twentieth century – Lord Denning.

Among the ranks of the lawyers who have considered the evidence, one interloper needs to be unmasked. In 1930 a book was published entitled *Who Moved the Stone?*, and it has been republished on numerous occasions. It was written by Frank

Morison, and it somehow became a common view that he was a lawyer – for example in *Evidence that Demands a Verdict* by Josh McDowell he was variously described as a lawyer, a professor, and a barrister (see pages 190, 208, 217). In fact he was none of these. Ironically he was not even Frank Morison either, as this was a pseudonym for Albert Henry Ross, a founder member and honorary fellow of the Institute of Incorporated Practitioners in Advertising. This does not in any way diminish the force of the book. Morison (we will continue to use his chosen name) set out to study the life of Jesus "with a very definite feeling that, if I may so put it, His History rested upon very insecure foundations" (1930, 2006, page 2). However, having studied in detail the evidence concerning the trial, death, and resurrection of Jesus, he concluded that "there may be, and, as the writer thinks, there certainly is, a deep and profoundly historical basis for the much disputed sentence in the Apostles Creed – "The third day he rose again from the dead" – words that, as a young Anglican, he had refused to utter (pages 223, 70).

SUMMARY

- Experts can give evidence as to their opinion as to matters which fall within their skill, training and experience.

- Eminent experts in the fields of palaeography, ancient history, and literature have commented positively on the reliability of the Gospel records.

- Although expert evidence would not be permitted from lawyers, eminent lawyers over the years have been convinced by the evidence about Jesus.

CHAPTER 16

Other Explanations

When you have eliminated the impossible,
whatever remains, however improbable,
must be the truth.

Sherlock Holmes[47]

When confronted with a civil claim, the defendant has a number of choices. He can admit the claim, either completely or in part, he can deny it, or he can "put the claimant to proof". As it is the claimant who must prove the claim on the balance of probabilities, the defendant does not need to put forward a detailed defence with an alternative version or interpretation of the facts for the judge. He can simply require the claimant to prove his claim. This usually happens in cases when the defendant does not actually know what happened – for example, when the defendant to an accident claim is a driver's insurance company and the driver himself is being uncooperative. If the insurance company has doubts whether the claim is valid, or simply does not know what happened, it will require the claimant to prove his claim to the satisfaction of the court.

However, in the majority of cases, defendants will put forward their own version of events. Putting a claimant to proof is a risky strategy, because once the judge is satisfied that the claimant is being honest, there will be no alternative explanation of the facts for the judge to consider. So in the vast majority of cases, a positive defence will be advanced – in our accident claim the defendant will suggest that the accident was actually the claimant's fault, someone else's fault, no one's fault (after all, some accidents just happen without anyone being at fault), or a combination of these.

In the same way, although it is possible simply to look at the evidence pointing to the conclusion that Jesus rose from the dead and to say "case proved", failing to consider other possible explanations of the facts would result in an unsatisfactory position all round. From the point of view of the sceptic, it would suggest that the claim is being prejudged. From the point of view of a neutral observer, it would suggest that justice is not being done. And from the point of view of many Christians, it would deprive them of the opportunity of saying that they have considered the alternative explanations and none of them are feasible. So we do need to consider some alternative explanations that have been put forward.

Before looking at these, there are two preliminary points which need to be made. The first is that there are so many theoretical explanations which have been put forward that it would be impossible to consider them all. As many of them are based on no evidence whatsoever, and indeed fly in the face of all the evidence, it is not actually necessary to consider them. Most of these explanations can be categorized under the heading "conspiracy theories", which we can consider together in general terms.

The second point is the need to consider "necessary" and "sufficient" conditions. A necessary condition is one which is required to produce a specific result. A sufficient condition is one which guarantees that result. So if I wish to take the 9.35 a.m. from Manchester to Euston, it is necessary for me to be on the platform ready to board the train by 9.34 a.m. (as the doors close forty-five seconds before it leaves). However, that is not sufficient for me to catch the train, as it is also necessary for the train to be there! These two necessary conditions are together sufficient – train plus punctual passenger equals actual journey. (A pedant might suggest that there are other necessary conditions here, such as the doors being open, the passenger actually boarding rather than collapsing with a heart attack and so on, but the general idea is clear.) We need to bear this in mind as we consider alternative explanations of the resurrection evidence. For such explanations to be *sufficient*, they will need to deal with at least the following issues:

- The empty tomb.

- The reports of resurrection appearances.

- The growth of the early church.

An explanation which deals only with one or two of these issues will be interesting, but not sufficient to deal with the whole of the evidence. What we are looking for is one explanation, or a combination of explanations, which will deal with all three issues.

In this chapter we shall examine the first group of explanations, which deals specifically with the empty tomb. The second group deals with the resurrection appearances, and the third with all three issues, and these we shall examine in our next chapter.

So, in logical sequence, we will consider the possibilities that:

- Jesus did not die.

- Jesus did die, but his body was not buried in a tomb.

- Jesus was buried in a tomb, but his body was stolen.

- Jesus' body remained and may still remain in the tomb.

- The resurrection appearances were hallucinations.

- The resurrection appearances were a result of cognitive dissonance.

- There was a conspiracy.

Jesus did not die

The first alternative explanation we must examine is that Jesus did not die on the cross but was mistakenly presumed dead. There is no evidence that this explanation was suggested at any point in the early life of the church, but it has been suggested much more recently, for example by Karl Venturini in the eighteenth century. It is suggested that Jesus passed out on the cross, but awoke in the tomb and subsequently met with his disciples who mistakenly believed that he had come back to life.

The major problem with this theory is that it is simply impossible to reconcile with the nature of the crucifixion. Even if we ignore completely the statements in the Gospels that Jesus was definitely dead, all accounts from outside the Bible are unanimous in stressing how painful and lethal Roman crucifixion was – Cicero described it as a most cruel and disgusting punishment (*Against Verres* 2.5.165). The idea that someone who, after being whipped and beaten, had spent several hours nailed to a cross by his hands or wrists and feet or ankles, and had been placed in a tomb, could somehow revive and do anything without considerable assistance is simply incredible.

Josephus refers in his *Life of Flavius Josephus* to three acquaintances that he persuaded Titus to reprieve – "he immediately commanded them to be taken down, and to have the greatest care taken of them, in order to aid their recovery; yet two of them died under the physician's hands, while the third recovered". If victims of crucifixion were unlikely to survive even when the greatest medical care was taken of them, they would stand no chance at all if placed in a tomb. For full details of the nature and effects of crucifixion, it is useful to refer to an article by William Edwards and others in the *Journal of the American Medical Association*[48] in 1986 which suggests that:

> the scourging produced deep stripelike lacerations and appreciable blood loss, and it probably set the stage for hypovolemic shock... the major pathophysiologic effect of crucifixion was an interference with normal respirations. Accordingly death resulted primarily from hypovolemic shock and exhaustion asphyxia. Modern medical interpretation of the evidence indicates that Jesus was dead when taken down from the cross.

Even if Jesus had – against all the odds – survived, there is no way in which he could have recovered without considerable help from others, and certainly no way in which he could have appeared to the disciples over the following days. He would not have been able to walk for a very long period.

All this is without the evidence of the Gospels – that Jesus was whipped before being crucified; that a spear was driven into his side resulting in a flow of blood and water; that he was definitely dead when taken down from the cross; that he was wrapped in graveclothes; and that the tomb was sealed with a large rock.

This explanation also fails to account for the resurrection appearances or the rise of the early church. It is not conceivable that anyone who had seen Jesus in this condition would have thought for a moment that he had been raised from the dead – they are much more likely to have called for the first-century equivalent of an ambulance!

So this explanation in fact explains nothing at all.

Jesus' body was not buried in a tomb

The second explanation is that Jesus did die on the cross but was not buried in an identifiable tomb. He was either left to "rot" on the cross, or was thrown into an unmarked burial pit, possibly with other crucifixion victims. Again, this is a relatively recent theory, propounded for example by Charles Guignebert in the early twentieth century.

At first sight, if we totally ignore the Gospels, this theory does have some basis – it was not normal for the victims of crucifixion to be given an honourable burial, and it was standard procedure for them to be left on the cross or thrown into a pit. However, in his *Wars of the Jews* Josephus stated that "the Jews used to take so much care of the burial of men, that they took down those that were condemned and crucified, and buried them before the going down of the sun". And the Gospel of John states (19:31) that the Jewish authorities did not want the bodies left on the crosses during the sabbath.

The major problem with this theory is that it cannot fit with what happened in the following days. If there had been any substance at all to this suggestion, it would have been an obvious riposte by both the Jewish and Roman authorities to the early Christian preaching. As we have seen, the message was simple – Jesus was dead and buried but had risen again. If the simple answer to this was "no, you are wrong, his body was thrown into a pit", then surely this answer would have been given immediately, and it would still have been possible to identify the pit. However, there is no hint that this was ever suggested.

Also, once again, this theory cannot account for the resurrection appearances. And it requires wholesale rejection of the detailed accounts in the Gospels of Jesus' burial. This theory does not explain the empty tomb; it ignores it. It is a hypothesis without any supporting evidence.

The body was stolen

We come now to a theory which is very much older – so old indeed that it is referred to in the Gospels (Matthew 28:11–15):

> While the women were on their way, some of the guards went into the city and reported to the chief priests everything that had happened. When the chief priests had met with the elders and devised a plan, they gave the soldiers a large sum of money, telling them, 'You are to say, "His disciples came during the night and stole him away while we were asleep." If this report gets to the governor, we will satisfy him and keep you out of trouble.' So the soldiers took the money and did as they were instructed. And this story has been widely circulated among the Jews to this very day.

It is highly unlikely that Matthew would have bothered to make the final "throw away" comment about the story still being in circulation if it was not true. So it seems as though this theory was raised almost as soon as the early Christians began their preaching.

Pausing here, the disciples would not be the only possible candidates as body snatchers. The Roman or Jewish authorities, or anonymous grave-robbers, could also be under suspicion. We can disregard the first two groups immediately – there is no reason why the authorities would take the body, and had they done so it would have been very simple for them to confirm that they had done so, or even produce the body, to refute the claim that Jesus had risen.

So, leaving aside for a moment the possibility of grave-robbers, the disciples are left as the only plausible suspects, but this possibility also evaporates as quickly as we try to grasp it. Why would the disciples steal the body? It had already been buried, so what else were they intending to do with a corpse? How, psychologically, could they have done this, having been thrown into disarray by the arrest, trial, and crucifixion of their leader? How, physically, could they have done this if, as stated in the Gospels, the tomb was guarded? How, morally, could they have gone on to preach that Jesus was alive if they had the ultimate skeleton in the cupboard? Why would they, in many cases, have gone to their deaths proclaiming that Jesus was alive, if they could have avoided this by admitting they knew what had happened to the body? As Sir Norman Anderson states, "The suggestion is impossible both psychologically and ethically" (1950, page 5).

This brings us finally to the possibility of grave-robbers. Such a suggestion would theoretically be possible, as this was a known phenomenon at the time. However, it would be a remarkable coincidence if robbers had stolen the body in the very short interval between its being placed in the tomb and the visits to the tomb – approximately thirty-six hours. Additionally, if the Gospels are to be believed, the body of Jesus was placed in a sealed tomb and the tomb was guarded, which would make it a very unattractive target for robbers. Also, the only items of any value in the tomb – the graveclothes and spices – were left behind when the body went, which would be surprising if robbery were the motive.

This is the first theory that would actually explain the empty tomb, were it not for the weaknesses in the theory once it is examined. Additionally, it again fails to account for the resurrection appearences and the preaching of the early church, but these considerations cast serious doubt on the possibility. And again it requires us totally to reject the Gospel accounts.

The body remained in the tomb

This, then, is the only remaining theory which can address the empty tomb – the theory that it was not empty at all. Either the disciples did not visit the tomb as claimed, and the Gospel stories are pure fabrication; or they went to the wrong tomb in their grief-stricken confusion.

This latter idea has been advanced, for example, by Professor Kirsopp Lake, who in a spectacular piece of selective quotation relies on Mark's account of a young man in the empty tomb saying to the women who had gone to anoint Jesus' body, "You are looking for Jesus the Nazarene, who was crucified. He is not here. See the place where they laid him" (Mark 16:6). Professor Lake comments: "and [he] probably pointed at the next tomb" (1907, pages 251–52). But he has neatly omitted the crucial words "He has risen" from the middle of this passage, which completely undermines his interpretation.

This theory founders for the same reasons as the non-burial theory. If Jesus' body was (and presumably still is, to this day) in a tomb, it is inconceivable that this would not have been pointed out as soon as the early Christians started causing trouble by saying "he has risen". There is no evidence at all that there was any suggestion that Jesus' body remained dead and buried – the only early suggestion was that it had been stolen. Why would this have been suggested if the body was available for all to see? These problems also arise in relation to the suggestion that Jesus' body was moved to a different tomb. If such removal had been unknown to the disciples, it would still have been known to his family (including James) or to the authorities.

Even if this theory had some merit, it would not explain the resurrection appearances and would require us completely to disregard the Gospel accounts (apart from selected extracts from Mark 16!).

SUMMARY

- To deal sufficiently with the evidence, other theories have to explain the empty tomb, the resurrection appearances, and the rise of the church.

- Theories to explain the empty tomb are that Jesus did not die on the cross, that he was not buried in a tomb, that his body was taken or stolen, and that his body remains in a tomb.

- All of these theories face very significant problems, and do not by themselves explain the resurrection appearances or the rise of the church.

CHAPTER 17

More Explanations

It is a capital mistake to theorize before one has data.
Insensibly, one begins to twist facts to suit theories,
instead of theories to suit facts.

Sherlock Holmes[49]

Having considered various theories which address the phenomenon of the empty tomb, we now turn to those which address the resurrection appearances.

There are really only three possibilities here – either the disciples were deceived by someone, or they invented the stories of the appearances, or they were simply and tragically mistaken. We will consider the first and second options later – as elements of conspiracy theories. First we will consider the mistake theory.

The resurrection appearances were hallucinations

Black's Medical Dictionary (page 293) defines hallucinations as:

> False perceptions arising without an adequate external stimulus, as opposed to illusions, which are misinterpretations of stimuli arising from an external object. Hallucinations come from "within", although the affected individual may see them as coming from "without". Nevertheless, they may occur at the same time as real perceptions, and may affect any sense (vision, hearing, smell, taste, touch, etc).

Causes include intense emotion or suggestion, sensory deprivation (for example lack of sleep) and disorders of the sense organs or central nervous system. *The British Medical Association Illustrated Medical Dictionary* confirms (page 359) that auditory hallucinations are a major symptom of schizophrenia, and may also be caused by bipolar disorder. Visual hallucinations are most often found in states of delirium brought on by a physical illness.

Studies over the years have reported widely differing numbers of people who admit to having experienced hallucinations – roughly 10% in 1895, over 14% in 1948, and almost 39% in 2000.[50]

It has been suggested that Jesus' disciples were predisposed to hallucinations – they were exhausted, stressed, and had just suffered a violent and unexpected bereavement. They felt guilty for abandoning Jesus (and, in Peter's case, denying him). It was therefore only natural that they would see and hear something and that this something would be interpreted as being Jesus.

This suggestion has not been advanced with great enthusiasm, and for good reason. Although hallucinations are not uncommon, the studies show that multi-modal hallucinations are much rarer. The reported appearances of Jesus all involved both sight and sound, and some involved touch as well. It would also be statistically so unlikely (in reality impossible) for all of the disciples to have experienced hallucinations at the same time. It would likewise be in reality impossible that they would have the same hallucinations on the same occasions, or that the hallucinations would persist for a specific period and then stop for all of them.

Finally, people who are not mentally ill tend not to believe that their hallucinations are real. I well remember as a teenager waking in the middle of the night to see very vividly my grandmother's head floating across the room (it had been her room before she died). Although at the time this was worryingly realistic, I was in no doubt that I had been hallucinating rather than actually seeing my dead grandmother's head! This is utterly different from the experiences of the disciples, who clearly believed that what they were seeing, hearing, and touching was Jesus himself.

Cognitive dissonance

A more plausible suggestion than simple hallucination is that the disciples were placed in a position of cognitive dissonance and were seeking to reconcile the conflict between their beliefs and the death of Jesus. By way of reminder, cognitive dissonance is the condition where someone experiences conflicting ideas simultaneously, and as a result seeks to alter one or more of the ideas so as to produce harmony. The disciples had come to believe that Jesus was the long-expected Messiah who had arisen to liberate God's people. They had devoted several years of their lives to following him. And now he was dead, rejected by the very people he had come to liberate, and executed by the people whose oppression he had been expected to destroy (the Romans). In order to try and make sense of this apparent contradiction, the disciples came to believe that Jesus was in fact alive – that he had been raised from the dead and that he was (despite appearances to the contrary) Israel's Messiah. They felt that Jesus was still with them, and either as hallucination or a rationalization of that inner feeling, or both, they began to spread the word that Jesus had risen from the dead. As Karen Armstrong puts it in her bestselling *A History of God* (page 98):

> Yet, despite the scandal of a Messiah who had died like
> a common criminal, his disciples could not believe
> that their faith in him had been misplaced. There were
> rumours that he had risen from the dead. Some said

that his tomb had been found empty three days after his crucifixion; others saw him in visions.

Although this suggestion is superficially attractive, it does not stand up to scrutiny. On a general level what happened to Jesus was completely irreconcilable with the Jewish expectation of their Messiah, while on a specific level the disciples had no expectation that Jesus would rise from the dead. N. T. Wright suggests that Jesus' crucifixion amounted to "the complete destruction of any messianic pretensions or possibilities... It said powerfully and irresistibly that he wasn't [the Messiah]" (2003, page 558). There were many other potential messiahs at the same time as the Christian message was being proclaimed, and no one thought to suggest that, despite being executed by the Romans, they were actually the Messiah. As we will see in the following chapter, the Gospels make it clear that, although Jesus had predicted his death and resurrection, the disciples simply did not understand what he was talking about. We recall how, when Peter rebuked Jesus for even suggesting it, he received an ever sharper rebuke in return: "Get behind me, Satan! You are a stumbling-block to me; you do not have in mind the concerns of God, but merely human concerns" (Matthew 16:23). Although there was a Jewish expectation of a general resurrection "at the last day" (see John 11:24), there was absolutely no expectation of a specific immediate resurrection of a Messiah.

So the disciples might have done a number of things in response to Jesus' death – they might have spread his ethical teaching, or tried to live out their lives as Jesus had taught them to do, and in this way they might have suggested that he somehow "lived on" through their teaching and living. But that is emphatically what they did not do. As we have seen, their very early preaching was focused entirely on Jesus' death and resurrection, and they spoke of the latter in the same terms and the same breath as the former. For them, the resurrection was as much hard fact as the crucifixion.

Finally, we must remind ourselves that neither hallucinations nor cognitive dissonance can account for the empty tomb.

There was a conspiracy

We have seen that none of the other theories suggested can, by itself, account for the empty tomb, the resurrection appearances, and the rise of the early church. The only theories which attempt to do so are conspiracy theories, and there is no shortage of these. Some of these are expressly fiction, for example *The Good Man Jesus and the Scoundrel Christ* by Philip Pullman, which expressly states "this is a story", even if it has nonetheless caused controversy among some Christians. Some are fiction with a suggestion that they are based on fact (for example *The Da Vinci Code*). And some are expressly said to be based on fact (for example *Holy Blood, Holy Grail*). It is impossible to even begin to examine all the theories which have been put forward over the years, but they tend to have similar characteristics:

- They identify a number of conspirators, often including Joseph of Arimathea, Mary Magdalene, Judas, and Jesus himself.

- They are very selective in their use of the Gospels to support the theory, while disregarding anything which runs counter to it.

- They attribute to the disciples either astonishing stupidity or astonishing duplicity.

- They are based on no actual evidence at all, but on speculation.

Of course, conspiracies do exist. For example, there is an unfortunate and increasing trend for drivers to "stage" accidents so as to make claims on their insurance policies. However, as with any claim the judge must decide where the truth lies on the balance of probabilities after assessing the evidence. A judge who accepts the suggestion that there has been a conspiracy based only on suspicion will find his judgment reversed on appeal, with sharp words of criticism by the appeal court.

A good example of a conspiracy theory is the suggestion that Jesus was given a drug on the cross to make it appear that he had died. He was then placed in the tomb, where he revived and was able to make his escape. Those involved in the conspiracy include Joseph of Arimathea (whose tomb it was), Mary Magdalene (who, it is suggested, subsequently married Jesus and bore his children), Pilate or someone else with sufficient authority to certify that Jesus was dead, and Jesus himself. Parts of the Gospels are cited as supporting evidence, for example Jesus asking for and drinking "wine vinegar" immediately before he died (Matthew 27:48–50; Mark 15:36–37; John 19:28–30), the surprisingly quick death of Jesus (Mark 15:44–45) and the fact that Jesus' legs were not broken, unlike those of the men crucified with him (John 19:31–33).

The weaknesses of this theory are apparent as soon as it is considered. First, it is simply not acceptable to extract parts of someone's evidence which support your case, totally out of context, while at the same time ignoring those parts which are hostile to your case. The Gospel accounts state specifically that Jesus was dead, and although his legs were not broken, the following verse states that his side was pierced with a spear resulting in a sudden flow of blood and water (John 19:34). Either the Gospel accounts cannot be trusted, in which case they cannot be used to support a theory such as this, or they can be trusted, in which case they do not support a theory such as this!

Second, if there was a conspiracy which involved the disciples, why would "clues" to the conspiracy such as the drinking of the wine vinegar be included in the Gospels, when they could perfectly easily have been left out?

Third, it is hard to imagine why Pontius Pilate would collude with such a conspiracy to secretly cancel the death penalty he himself had imposed, with the serious risk to his authority and position if the conspiracy was discovered.

Fourth, if the disciples were involved in the conspiracy, they were both dishonest and foolish in the extreme to then start preaching Jesus' resurrection, with the resulting persecution and even death. If they were not involved in the conspiracy, how did they become convinced that Jesus had risen from the dead?

Fifth, the involvement of Jesus in the conspiracy runs counter to everything we know about his character from the Gospels.

In short, this theory is a "work of historical conjecture", based on no actual evidence and a considerable amount of supposition.

If the same rigorous analysis is applied to any "conspiracy theory", however sensationally it may be presented, it will quickly determine whether there is any actual evidence (as opposed to supposition) supporting the theory, and whether the theory can account adequately for the three necessary conditions which we have identified – the empty tomb, the resurrection appearances, and the dramatic growth of the early church.

As noted in the previous chapter, there are a huge number of theoretical explanations which have been suggested over the years, the most recent being a fascinating hypothesis involving the Turin Shroud. For readers who are interested in considering these, a number are analyzed in Appendix 3, where we ask how, if at all, they account for the evidence which we have considered thus far. It is suggested that this approach can be used to analyze any alternative theories which are put forward, to decide whether they may have any merit.

SUMMARY

- Theories of hallucination or cognitive dissonance face very significant problems and cannot explain the empty tomb.

- No single theory can explain the empty tomb, the resurrection appearances, and the rise of the early church, except conspiracy theories.

- When conspiracy theories are examined carefully, it is clear that they are based on speculation only, not on evidence.

CHAPTER 18

The Testimony of Jesus

*I was a prophecy before; but the things that I foretold
have come to pass. So it is just as well I have changed,
or I would have become a History! A dry-as-dust
History![51]*

Generally "previous consistent statements" by a witness need
to be treated with great care. These are statements made by the
witness before giving evidence, which turn out to be consistent
with that evidence. The reason for such caution is obvious –
there is a real danger that the statements may be self-serving
and made to strengthen the evidence that is coming later. For
this reason, in civil cases a party requires permission of the
court to rely on such statements (in England an Wales, pursuant
to Section 6(2)(a) of the Civil Evidence Act). However, such
permission is not required where the statements are being relied
upon to rebut a suggestion of recent fabrication of evidence
by the witness (Section 6(2)(b)). For example, if following a
collision one of the drivers tells all of his friends that the other
driver failed to stop at a red light, the court would need to give
permission for these statements to be relied upon as evidence.
However, if the other driver was suggesting that this story had
recently been concocted in an attempt to avoid liability after
legal proceedings had begun, the first driver would not need
permission to rely on the statements as evidence that he had
been telling the same story from the outset.

We need to apply the same principles to statements made by Jesus before his death, and to proceed with great caution. If Jesus was indeed who the early church portrayed him to be – the Son of God who died and rose again – then we would expect him to have said things about this while he was alive, and such statements would be evidence that the early church had not invented the idea of his resurrection. On the other hand, there would also be a very strong incentive for the church to "project back" supposed statements of Jesus which supported their claims that Jesus had risen.

In order to try and assess whether we should give any weight to statements which the Gospel writers attribute to Jesus, it is first necessary to look at the statements themselves in context. Across the Gospels, there are eight relevant ones.

1. The sign of Jonah

In Matthew 12:39–40 Jesus is recorded as saying: "A wicked and adulterous generation asks for a sign! But none will be given it except the sign of the prophet Jonah. For as Jonah was three days and three nights in the belly of a huge fish, so the Son of Man will be three days and three nights in the heart of the earth."

Luke also records the saying in 11:29–30, but instead of referring to three days and nights, he records Jesus saying "For as Jonah was a sign to the Ninevites, so also will the Son of Man be to this generation."

2. Jesus and Peter

Matthew, Mark, and Luke all record Jesus asking his disciples who other people think he is, and who they think he is. Peter responds that he is "the Messiah", and Jesus goes on to "teach them that the Son of Man must suffer many things and be rejected by the elders, the chief priests and the teachers of the law, and that he must be killed and after three days rise again" (Mark 8:27–31).

Peter then rebuked Jesus, as we have seen when considering Peter's testimony.

The parallel passages in Matthew (16:21) and Luke (9:22) say "on the third day" rather than "after three days".

3. Second prediction to the disciples

Matthew and Mark record an incident after the "transfiguration" and the healing of a boy with a demon when Jesus again predicted that "the Son of Man is going to be delivered into the hands of men. They will kill him, and on the third day he will be raised to life" (Matthew 17:22–23).

Mark again says "after three days" (9:31–32). Matthew goes on to say that the disciples were "filled with grief". Mark records that they "did not understand what he meant and were afraid to ask him about it".

4. Third prediction

Matthew, Mark, and Luke record a third incident when Jesus told the disciples, "We are going up to Jerusalem, and the Son of Man will be delivered over to the chief priests and the teachers of the law. They will condemn him to death and will hand him over to the Gentiles to be mocked and flogged and crucified. On the third day he will be raised to life!" (Matthew 20:18–19).

Luke adds that "the disciples did not understand any of this … they did not know what he was talking about" (Luke 18:34). Matthew and Mark both follow this prediction with an incident where James and John (or their mother, on their behalf) asked to sit on Jesus' right and left "in your glory".

5. Going to Galilee

Matthew and Mark record Jesus predicting, in the context of his prediction of Peter's betrayal, that "after I have risen, I will go ahead of you into Galilee" (Matthew 26:32; Mark 14:28).

6. The Temple

John records the Jews asking for a miraculous sign, and his reply: " 'Destroy this temple, and I will raise it again in three days' ... But the temple he had spoken of was his body. After he was raised from the dead, his disciples recalled what he had said. Then they believed the Scripture and the words that Jesus had spoken" (John 2:19–22).

7. The Temple again

Both Matthew and Mark record that in Jesus' trial witnesses came forward to testify that Jesus had said, "I am able to destroy the temple of God and rebuild it in three days" (Matthew 26:61) and "I will destroy this temple made with human hands and in three days will build another, not made with hands" (Mark 14:58).

8. Grief and joy

In John 16:16–22 Jesus is recorded as telling his disciples, "In a little while you will see me no more, and then after a little while you will see me." The disciples did not understand this, so Jesus went on to say "you will weep and mourn while the world rejoices. You will grieve, but your grief will turn to joy ... I will see you again and you will rejoice..."

What can we say about these statements? On the negative side, there are clearly inconsistencies between some of the different accounts where they are recorded in more than one Gospel. Some may be easily reconciled, for example the disciples being both filled with grief and not understanding what Jesus said – the two are not inconsistent. Others cannot be so easily reconciled, such as the difference between "on the third day" and "after three days" (though this may be a result of the Gospel writers using different phrases to render Jesus' reference to a brief period of time).

However, on the positive side, there are a number of things which can be said:

• Although different combinations of sayings are recorded in each Gospel, each Gospel records two or more sayings. They are therefore consistent at a generalized level.

• As we have already noted, the fact that witnesses give differing evidence does not necessarily mean that the evidence is false or that it cannot be relied upon. It may be said that the differences between the Gospel accounts (both the different combinations of sayings and the differences in individual accounts) strengthen the evidence, in the sense that collusion between the writers is ruled out. Obviously this point cannot be pursued too far in relation to wildly inconsistent evidence, but these statements are not in that category.

• Where the reaction of the disciples is recorded it is one of incomprehension, grief or (in the case of Peter) an outright rebuke of Jesus. This is entirely consistent with the statements being genuine. As we have already noted in relation to Peter, stories showing the weaknesses of the disciples (who became the leaders in the early church) are much more likely to be authentic than stories showing them to be strong and wise. In most cases, there is no attempt to cover up the disciples' reaction, which would have been very easy if the accounts were being fabricated.

- The accounts indirectly corroborate each other. This is most notable in the saying relating to the temple. The saying is only directly attributed to Jesus in John; witnesses attribute it to him in Matthew and Mark. The two accounts together make a complete and coherent whole. Also, as we have already seen, Matthew and John record appearances of the risen Jesus to the disciples in Galilee, but Matthew and Mark record Jesus' predictions of those meetings. Again, the Gospels corroborate each other.

- The sayings are unlike anything which appears elsewhere in the New Testament. Scholars often apply a criterion of "dissimilarity" to the Gospels – if something in the Gospels is similar to what was being taught in the early church, then it is less likely to be authentic and more likely to be "projected back" by the Gospel writers. Once again this point cannot be pursued too far, because it is totally obvious that there would be a considerable overlap between the teaching of Jesus and that of the early church. However, it is noteworthy that the "sign of Jonah" and the references to Jesus destroying and rebuilding the temple are completely absent from the rest of the New Testament.

Taking all these factors into consideration, and applying considerable caution for the reasons already discussed, we can be reasonably confident that Jesus did predict his resurrection on a number of occasions, even if we cannot be as certain about the exact words which he used. Once Jesus had risen from the dead, the prophecies were recalled and became a part of his story, and subsequently of history as they were recorded in the Gospels.

SUMMARY

- If Jesus was the Son of God, we would expect him to predict his resurrection.

- According to the Gospels, Jesus predicted his resurrection on at least seven occasions.

- We must exercise considerable caution with these predictions, which are self-serving for the early church.

- However, there are good reasons to accept in general terms that the predictions are authentic.

PART 3

REACHING A VERDICT

CHAPTER 19

Summing Up

It is also more in accordance with a healthy faith to believe that truth is not served by the suppression of inquiry, but that it flourishes in the fullest exercise of the critical faculties with which man has been endowed.

Sir Frederic Kenyon (1940, page 29)

After the evidence has been given, and before the verdict is reached, the case is summed up. In some cases the evidence which has been given turns out to be very different from that which was expected, and the summing-up will give the advocates the opportunity of formulating their case as best they can in light of that evidence. In other cases, the evidence may have revealed no surprises, and the summing-up gives the advocates the opportunity to draw attention to the points which they consider to be important.

In civil cases, the advocates each sum up in their "closing submissions" to the judge, and not infrequently they will each invite the judge to decide that their client's evidence is correct and that of the opponent is false. Each will put forward reasons to support these submissions – for example the number of witnesses, the consistency of the evidence, the consistency of the party's conduct with the evidence he has given, the likelihood of that version of events being true, and so on. In criminal trials the prosecution and defence advocates sum up in a similar manner but, before the jury retires to consider its verdict, the judge then sums up for them the nature of the issues which they have to decide and the evidence which may assist them in doing so.

The summing-up may be very lengthy or very short, depending on the nature of the case and the skill of the advocate – legal legend has it that in one case a barrister summed up by saying, "The claimant is an honest man. Accept his evidence and allow the claim." To which the judge responded, "He isn't and I don't. Claim dismissed!" Most summings-up, and judgments, are rather more detailed than that!

In the same way, it is helpful to sum up the issues and evidence which have been considered in relation to Jesus. This is not intended to replace a detailed consideration of the issues (so if you have jumped to this chapter, please go back and read all the others!), but it is intended to identify the key issues concerning the method to be applied and the evidence which has been considered. Summaries have appeared at the end of each chapter, and these summaries are now reproduced as a summing-up. As will immediately be apparent, this is more like the summing-up of a judge in a criminal trial than that of advocates, because of the way the argument has progressed. It is put forward as a structure which can be used to work through the issues, how they are to be considered, and the evidence, with a view to enabling readers to decide for themselves what verdict they will reach.

1. Jesus

- There is a wide spectrum of views about Jesus.
- Many believe that the church has conspired to hide the truth about Jesus.
- We will focus on the central Christian claim about Jesus – that he rose from the dead.

167

2. *History*

- The story of Jesus should be considered as history, not myth or legend.

- The claims about Jesus go beyond history, but this does not mean that we cannot analyse the historical evidence.

3. *Proof*

- In considering the resurrection of Jesus, we are asking whether it can be proved.

- The onus is on those suggesting the resurrection to prove that it did occur.

- Very cogent evidence will be required.

4. *Evidence*

- The number and age of New Testament manuscripts compares extremely favourably with other ancient texts.

- The writers of the New Testament wrote as, or reflecting the testimony of, eyewitnesses.

5. *The Judge*

- We need to identify and set aside any prejudices we have about Jesus.

- One such prejudice is simply to believe all that the Bible says.

- Another prejudice is that Jesus was simply an ordinary man.

6. *Starting point*

- Despite Roman occupation, first-century Judaism remained monotheistic, centred on the temple, with a strong messianic hope.

- From this emerged the early church, which reinterpreted the fundamentals of Jewish belief.
- *Something unexpected happened* to produce this result.

7. Paul

- Paul was a devout Jew, involved in persecuting Christians.
- *Something unexpected happened* to change him into a Christian preacher, theologian, missionary and martyr.
- Both he and the writer of Acts attributed the change to seeing the risen Jesus.

8. James

- James, Jesus' brother, was sceptical about Jesus during his lifetime.
- *Something unexpected happened* which led him to become a leader of the early church, and a martyr for his faith.
- The only plausible explanation for this change is that given by Paul – James had an experience of the risen Jesus.

9. Peter

- The Gospel records show Peter as someone who lacked understanding and faith, and who denied Jesus.
- *Something unexpected happened* which resulted in him becoming a major leader and preacher in the early church, who died for his faith in Jesus.
- There are several sources indicating that he changed by meeting the risen Jesus.

10. No body

- Despite claims to the contrary, there is no certainty about the location of Jesus' tomb, and his body is missing; this contrasts with other significant religious leaders.

- *Something unexpected happened* which meant that these questions were of no interest to the early church.

- The obvious explanation of this is their belief that Jesus had risen from the dead.

11. The early church

- *Something unexpected happened* which led to the birth and explosive growth of the early church.

- This cannot be explained by any military or social factors, or by the continuing leadership of its "founder".

- The preaching, practices, and response to persecution of the early church are consistent only with a central belief in the resurrection of Jesus.

12. Evidence outside the New Testament

- Non-Christian writers in the first and early second centuries confirm a number of facts about Jesus' life and death, and the beliefs of the early church.

- There is no explicit reference by these writers to the resurrection.

- The earliest Christian writers refer consistently to Jesus' resurrection.

13. The Gospels

- The four New Testament Gospels were a new genre of writing.

- A number of challenges have been raised to the historical reliability of the Gospels, each of which can be answered.

- At the very least, the Gospels can be relied upon to

corroborate other evidence. At the very best, they comprise four independent eyewitness accounts.

14. *The Gospels' Resurrection Accounts*

- At first, the four Gospel accounts of the resurrection seem so inconsistent as to be unbelievable.

- However, on closer examination, there are many points which suggest that they are essentially accurate accounts of the witnesses.

- At the very least, the accounts can be relied upon to corroborate other evidence. At the very best, they comprise four independent eyewitness accounts.

15. *Expert evidence*

- Experts can give evidence as to their opinion on matters which fall within their skill, training, and experience.

- Eminent experts in the fields of palaeography, ancient history, and literature have commented positively on the reliability of the Gospel records.

- Although expert evidence would not be permitted from lawyers, eminent lawyers over the years have been convinced by the evidence about Jesus.

16. *Other explanations*

- To deal sufficiently with the evidence, other theories have to explain the empty tomb, the resurrection appearances, and the rise of the church.

- Theories to explain the empty tomb are that Jesus did not die on the cross, that he was not buried in a tomb, that his body was taken or stolen, and that his body remains in a tomb.

- All of these theories face very significant problems, and do not by themselves explain the resurrection appearances or the rise of the church.

17. More explanations

- Theories of hallucination or cognitive dissonance face very significant problems and cannot explain the empty tomb.

- No single theory can explain the empty tomb, the resurrection appearances, and the rise of the early church, except conspiracy theories.

- When conspiracy theories are examined carefully, it is clear that they are based on speculation only, not on evidence.

18. The Testimony of Jesus

- If Jesus was the Son of God, we would expect him to predict his resurrection.

- According to the Gospels, Jesus predicted his resurrection on at least seven occasions.

- We must exercise considerable caution with these predictions, which are self-serving for the early church.

- However, there are good reasons to accept in general terms that the predictions are authentic.

Verdict

It is now for you, the reader, to judge for yourself:

Having considered all the evidence, am I satisfied that there is very cogent evidence that Jesus rose from the dead?

This may be a very easy decision to reach, and judges are often able to give an immediate "extempore" judgment at the end of the submissions made to them. Or it may be a more difficult decision, requiring reconsideration of some parts of the evidence. If necessary, judges are encouraged to take time to reach their decision, and for this reason they will "reserve" their judgment to a future date.

What is essential is that a decision be reached, and judges have in the past been criticized by the Court of Appeal for failing to produce a judgment within a reasonable time. The longer a judgment is left, the harder it is to reach, so unless the reader is able to come to an immediate decision, I would recommend setting aside a specific period of time to consider the evidence carefully and to reach a final decision: did Jesus rise from the dead?

CHAPTER 20

Jesus – So What?

After more than 700 hours of studying this subject, and thoroughly investigating its foundation, I have come to the conclusion that the resurrection of Jesus Christ is one of the "most wicked, vicious, heartless hoaxes ever foisted upon the minds of men, or it is the most fantastic fact of history".

Josh McDowell (1981, 1998, page 179)

Having reached a decision as to the facts, the task of the judge is still not complete, because he needs to go on to consider the consequences of that decision. Sometimes the consequences are obvious: if a claimant alleges that the defendant reversed into his stationary car but the judge decides that in fact the claimant drove into the rear of the defendant's stationary car, then the claim will be dismissed and the only questions left will relate to the legal costs and who has to pay them.

On other occasions, a decision on the facts is only the beginning of a whole series of other issues. There may be issues of legal liability; if the judge decides that the claimant carefully pulled out of a side road to turn right in front of a queue of stationary traffic, and collided with a motorcycle which was lawfully overtaking that queue, then who is legally at fault? There may be issues of contributory negligence; even if the claimant succeeds, he may face a percentage reduction because of his own actions, for example if he was not wearing a seat belt. There may be issues of causation; is it possible to suffer whiplash injury in an impact occurring below a certain speed?

There may be issues as to the damages a claimant can recover; is the loss foreseeable? Is it too remote?

Similar principles apply after we have reached our decision whether Jesus rose from the dead. If we have decided that he did not, then the consequences will be simple – we can walk away from the issue, perhaps agreeing that it is a wicked, vicious, heartless hoax, and that Christians must be particularly gullible. If we really cannot decide one way or the other, then we may wish to take some more time to consider a decision and perhaps do some further research. But if we decide that Jesus did rise from the dead, what are the consequences? Is this just a unique and fascinating historical anomaly, to be filed mentally with other quite interesting facts? I suggest not. I suggest that such an extraordinary event in history requires any serious enquirer to think very carefully about its meaning.

The early Christians very quickly reached their own conclusions about the meaning of Jesus' resurrection, and although this is not a book about theology, it is worthwhile spending a little time looking at their conclusions, given that they were the people who had lived with Jesus and who claimed to be witnesses to his resurrection. We can do so under two headings – theory and practice.

Theory

In a passage which we have already considered (1 Corinthians 15), Paul makes some very blunt statements about the importance of the resurrection for Christians. He says (verses 13–19, 30):

> If there is no resurrection of the dead, then not even
> Christ has been raised. And if Christ has not been
> raised, our preaching is useless and so is your faith. More
> than that, we are then found to be false witnesses about
> God ... if Christ has not been raised, your faith is futile;
> you are still in your sins. Then those also who have fallen

asleep in Christ are lost. If only for this life we have hope in Christ, we are of all people most to be pitied… And as for us, why do we endanger ourselves every hour?

For Paul, there is a simple binary choice. Either Jesus has been raised from the dead, in which case Christians have been saved from their sins, their faith is well placed, they have a hope beyond death, and their preaching and testimony are valid. Or Jesus has not been raised from the dead, in which case Christians are deluded, lost in sin, false witnesses, and without hope. There is no "third way", no "wiggle room", no diplomatic compromise. It is a multiple-choice question to which candidates must answer yes or no. And Paul goes on to say (to paraphrase Bill Shankly), "Some people believe the resurrection is a matter of life and death. I am very disappointed with that attitude. I can assure you it is much, much more important than that." (Shankly, of course, was referring to football rather than the resurrection.) Jesus is said by Paul to be the "firstfruits", and so those who belong to him will also be raised to life: "…we will all be changed – in a flash, in the twinkling of an eye, at the last trumpet. For the trumpet will sound, the dead will be raised imperishable, and we will be changed … then the saying that is written will come true: 'Death has been swallowed up in victory'" (1 Corinthians 15:51–54).

This is the Christian's ultimate reply to those who look at all the injustice and suffering in the world – one day there will be final judgment, not like the judgments of fallible (and sometimes corrupt) earthly judges, but a perfect judgment by the all-knowing God of righteousness and mercy. Wrongs will be righted and those who have managed to evade justice will finally be brought to account.

But there is more, much more to the belief of the early church about Jesus' resurrection than a belief in life beyond death, much more than "pie in the sky when you die". This is summed up in Paul's words in Romans 1:4 that Jesus "was declared with power to be the Son of God, by his resurrection from the dead: Jesus Christ our Lord". This is a succinct statement of three key beliefs about Jesus:

1. He was the Messiah. We have already considered the nature of the Jewish hope for a Messiah to liberate them from their Roman oppressors. The early church believed that Jesus was the Messiah, even though the Romans were very much still in control. They came to understand the nature of Jesus' messiahship in a different way: he had died and risen to liberate people from everything which corrupts their lives and alienates them from God – what Christians call "sin". He died and rose again to break down the barriers between people, between the sexes, the races, and the social classes (see Galatians 3:28), and between people and God, whether those people are part of the Jewish race or not (see Ephesians 2).

2. He was the Lord. As N. T. Wright points out, "When Paul says 'Jesus is Lord', it is clear that he meant that Caesar was not" (2000, page 98). Beginning with Augustus, Roman emperors divinized their predecessors, meaning that they were considered, literally, to be the son of a god. Proclaiming Jesus as Lord was to say that Christians owed their first loyalty to Jesus, not to Caesar. The Jews believed that the Messiah would inaugurate the rule of God's kingdom on earth. The Christians believed that as well, but again understood it in a very different way – God's kingdom was not to be found in a particular territory ruled by a king appointed by God, but was to be found in the lives of Christians living throughout the world, owing their first allegiance to Jesus and living out his kingdom values of righteousness and love. Indeed, the writings of the Roman historians and politicians we have considered bear witness to the fact that the early

Christians lived very distinct lives characterized by love and commitment to God and to each other.

3. He was God. The early Christians believed that Jesus was the unique Son of God, and by this they meant that he was in a unique way revealing God to the world. This was, and remains, a mystery, in the sense that we cannot fully understand it – how can Jesus be referred to as the Son of God and yet also *be* God? The Trinity is nowhere in the New Testament stated as an abstract doctrine, but it runs like a golden thread throughout it.[52] And so our ultimate questions about life are answered: Is there a God? Yes! Is he interested in people? Yes! Is there more to life than our three score years and ten? Yes! How can we know all this? Because Jesus has risen. And so Paul can tell his readers that "you know that your labour in the Lord is not in vain" (1 Corinthians 15:58).

The early church did not believe in a Jesus who was simply a great teacher, giving them wisdom to live by; nor in a Jesus who simply lived a life of love and holiness, setting them an example to follow; nor in a Jesus who simply died, a martyr for what was right. They believed in a Jesus who was the Messiah, who saved them from all that corrupted them and alienated them from God; in a Jesus who was Lord, to whom they gave their first allegiance; and in a Jesus who was God, who guarantees to those who choose to accept his lordship new life, beginning now and continuing beyond death.

Practice

In addition to these beliefs of the early church about Jesus, the other emphasis we find in the New Testament is on the way in which the lives of the early Christians were changed. We see this immediately after the risen Jesus appeared to them

– the disciples' sadness was replaced with joy and their fear with confidence. Peter, who had denied Jesus, was restored by the risen Jesus. The book of Acts is essentially a book about changed lives – the lives of the disciples, boldly proclaiming the risen Jesus in the face of hostility and persecution; the lives of individuals of different nationalities who were changed as they believed in Jesus; the lives of people who came together in love to support each other financially and in many other ways; the lives of people who experienced miracles of healing, and more. Paul's letters often begin with theological discussion but go on to discuss the way in which his readers are living out their faith – lives of love, joy, peace, patience, kindness, goodness, faithfulness, gentleness and self-control (Galatians 5:22–23). He was under no illusion that these early Christian groups had no problems, and much of his writings addresses those issues, but it is always done on the basis that the Christians have been changed because of what Jesus has done, and so by the power of the Holy Spirit they can lead changed lives.

Joining the dots

We have considered separately the theory and practice of the early church, but in reality they were simply two sides of the same coin, and this is seen in Paul's words, "I want to know Christ – yes, to know the power of his resurrection" (Philippians 3:10).

For the early church, Jesus' resurrection was not just an interesting fact or a theological talking point, so much head knowledge, but the focal point of God's power to change lives, something that could be experienced as personal knowledge.

And this has continued throughout history: although the church has much to be ashamed of (the crusades, the inquisition, the Wars of Religion, and more), wherever there has been authentic Christian faith lives have been changed: criminals have turned away from crime; addicts have been freed from addictions; selfish, self-centred individuals have become selfless and generous. In the memorable words of a Christian in Wales in the early twentieth century: "Whether he turned water into wine or not I do not know; but in my own house I have seen him turn beer into furniture."[53]

This is in fact the final piece of evidence for Jesus' resurrection – the changed lives of people who have encountered the risen Jesus. This is not evidence susceptible to analysis in a court in the same way as the other evidence we have been considering, because although a court could observe the change in someone's behaviour, it could not observe the catalyst for that change within the person. This kind of evidence can only truly be observed by personal experience – by individuals deciding for themselves to put their faith in the risen Jesus and to allow the Holy Spirit to change them from the inside out. Throughout history, millions of people of different gender, colour, nationality, religion, social class, age, and political outlook have done this, but the decision remains an intensely personal one. Even those who have concluded that Jesus' resurrection is "the most fantastic fact of history" are not obliged to take the further step of putting their trust in Jesus. Both Jesus and his followers made it crystal clear that it is a costly decision, because giving first allegiance to Jesus necessarily means that we cannot give first allegiance to ourselves and our own desires and wishes. Ultimately, there is a simple question to ask: do we want to trust in our own power to live our life, or to trust in the power which raised Jesus from the dead (Ephesians 1:19–20)? Simple to ask, but it may be difficult to answer.

Even so, having considered all the evidence and reached this point, each reader should, I believe, answer the question for themselves. Only then can they say (as judges never do!), "Case closed!"

Appendix 1

The Da Vinci Code and Other Modern Gnostic Myths

The publication of Dan Brown's novel *The Da Vinci Code* in 2003 led to massive controversy. Although that controversy has now largely passed into history, it is worth examining because it is an excellent example of the way in which challenges to orthodox beliefs about Jesus can become firmly established despite lacking any real foundation.

The underlying premise of the book is that the secret of Jesus' bloodline (the real "Holy Grail") has been preserved over the centuries by a secret organization called the Priory of Sion, whose members included Leonardo da Vinci. In the story codes and puzzles are intermingled with a murdering monk and secret rituals.

The book is only a novel of course, yet right at the start it boldly states this under the title *Fact*: "All descriptions of artwork, architecture, documents and secret rituals in this novel are accurate." Many readers have not only taken this statement at face value, but have gone on unthinkingly to extend it, concluding that the facts underlying the conspiracy at the heart of the book are true. Those "facts" are explained by one of the characters, Sir Leigh Teabing, a British Royal historian:

1. Until the Council of Nicea in AD 325 Jesus was viewed as a mortal prophet, not as the Son of God.

2. Jesus' establishment as Son of God was officially proposed and voted on at Nicea, and was agreed by a "relatively close vote".

3. Therefore it was the pagan Roman Emperor Constantine who turned Jesus into a deity, and did so for political reasons.

4. Jesus' life was recorded by thousands of his followers, and more than eighty gospels were considered for inclusion in the New Testament. Constantine commissioned and financed a new Bible, omitting the gospels which showed Jesus' human traits. Earlier gospels were outlawed and destroyed.

5. Some of these gospels survived, e.g. in the Dead Sea Scrolls and at Nag Hammadi.

6. History has never had a definitive version of the Bible.

7. Jesus was married to Mary Magdalene – "it's a matter of historical record".

In fact, all of these statements are false, and based on little if any "evidence" (see below). Not even the descriptions of artwork, architecture and so on are accurate – for example the Louvre pyramid is not constructed of 666 panes of glass (666 being the "number of Satan"). The precise number varies depending on whether one reads information from the Louvre itself or from the architects, but neither suggest that it is 666.

However, fans of the novel are reluctant to abandon their view that it is true, even when presented with hard evidence to the contrary. This was demonstrated in a fascinating documentary

The Grail Trail broadcast by ITV in September 2005. In the programme three aficionados of the book were taken to various locations referred to in the text, and met with experts on the subjects involved (for example, the history of the legend of the Holy Grail). Despite overwhelming proof that the factual basis of the conspiracy was completely unfounded, and despite the evidence of their own eyes that the descriptions of artwork and architecture were not all true, two of them continued to assert that the underlying idea of the book was true. It was as though they wanted to believe its truth (even though it is only a novel) so much that they were prepared to disregard the evidence – a clear example of cognitive dissonance.

The idea that the church has conspired over the centuries to conceal the real truth about Jesus is not a new idea. History has seen a multitude of books (and, more recently, television programmes) alleging to have uncovered the "real truth" about Jesus. One only has to walk into a bookshop today to find bestsellers including *Holy Blood, Holy Grail*. This was, in fact, referred to in *The Da Vinci Code*, and Leigh Teabing's name is derived from those of two of the authors of *Holy Blood* – Leigh and Baigent (of which Teabing is an anagram). Indeed Leigh and Baigent sued Dan Brown's publisher for damages for breach of copyright. That claim failed, and in a judgment which became better known when it was discovered that he had placed a coded message within it, Mr Justice Peter Smith described some of the ideas in *Holy Blood* as being "at the far end of conjecture" (Baigent & Leigh -v- Random House Group Ltd [2006] EWHC 719(Ch), para 46), the book having been described by its own authors as "a work of historical conjecture". The judgment was upheld by the Court of Appeal ([2007] EWCA Civ 247). Smith J. also said in his judgment (para 81), referring to *The Da Vinci Code*:

> Of course merely because an author of fiction describes matters as being factually correct does not mean that

they are factually correct. It is a way of blending fact and fiction together to create that well known model "faction". The lure of apparent genuineness makes the books and the films more receptive to the readers/ audiences. The danger of course is that the faction is all that large parts of the audience read and they accept it as truth.

In Appendix 3 we consider *Holy Blood, Holy Grail* and some other recent books about Jesus in the light of the evidence which we have considered in this book.

Returning to Teabing's seven "facts", the true position is as follows:

1. Christians had accepted the divinity of Jesus at a relatively early stage. That is clear from Paul's letters, which are accepted as having been written in the middle of the first century. There are numerous direct references to Jesus being the Son of God in the Gospels. It was also accepted that Jesus was both man and God – this can be seen from the early Christian writings from the end of the first century onwards, in addition to the New Testament writings. However, there was some disagreement as to Jesus' relationship with God the Father. A group led by Arius argued that Jesus was subordinate to the Father, rather than being "of one substance" with him.

2. The Council of Nicea was called by Emperor Constantine to resolve this issue. He invited all the bishops in the empire. Between 250 and 318 attended. When the Council voted, the Arian position was rejected. The precise voting figures are unknown, but it is clear that only two or three voted in favour of the

Arian position, with 99% voting in favour of the "one substance" view which now appears in the Nicene creed. So there was no vote on Jesus' "establishment as Son of God", nor a "relatively close vote".

3. Accordingly, Constantine did not "turn Jesus into a deity".

4. It is correct to note that other gospels were written, but most scholars agree that they were written much later than those in the New Testament – see chapter 13. There is no evidence to suggest that Jesus' life was recorded by thousands of his followers, and the total number of gospels which have been discovered is significantly less than eighty. Constantine did not commission a new Bible. The Gospels in the New Testament show Jesus as having more human traits than those not in the New Testament – they show him weeping, getting tired, becoming angry, being thirsty, and so on.

5. The Dead Sea Scrolls do not include any gospels at all. The gospels found at Nag Hammadi are believed by most scholars to post-date the Gospels in the New Testament, and they portray Jesus in a manner consistent with Gnostic beliefs, as a mystical figure. (Gnostic beliefs are too complex for detailed consideration here.)

6. The church had accepted the majority of the books now in the New Testament by AD 200. The final composition of the New Testament was acknowledged by the end of the fourth century. The East-Syrian Nestorian church and the Ethiopian church adopted different lists of books (22 and 35 respectively), but both of these include the four Gospels and no other gospels. (See the entries for

'Bible' and 'Canon' in the *Oxford Companion to the Bible* for full details.)

7. There is no evidence at all that Jesus was married to Mary Magdalene. The nearest suggestion is found in the Gospel of Philip. There it states:

Christ loved her more than all the disciples and used to kiss her often on the mouth. [The word 'mouth' is incomplete in the surviving manuscripts, but is considered the most likely text.] The rest of the disciples were offended by it and expressed disapproval. They said to him, "Why do you love her more than all of us?"

Even if this were accepted as being an accurate record, it would actually disprove the suggestion of Jesus' marriage, because if he had been married to Mary the disapproval of the disciples would make no sense. But there is no reason to accept the record as accurate – the gospel is believed to have been written in the third century.

Appendix 2

The Talpiot Tomb

The tomb was initially uncovered in the East Talpiot area of Jerusalem in 1980, but before it was fully excavated it was looted. It contained ten ossuaries, which contain skeletons, and other skeletons were found on niches and on the floor. It has been estimated that the tomb may have held as many as thirty-five people. The claim that the tomb is that of Jesus and his family is based on (1) the inscriptions on some of the ossuaries, (2) probability based on the names in the inscriptions and (3) DNA evidence. In brief, the contentious issues are these:

1. One ossuary is said to bear the inscription "Yeshua bar Yehosef" (Jesus, son of Joseph). However, the inscription of the name Jesus (Yeshua) is unclear, and many experts question whether the name is Jesus. For example, Stephen Pfann, President of the University of the Holy Land, suggests that "Hanun" is a more likely reading. If it is not Yeshua, the whole theory collapses.

2. Another ossuary bears the inscription "Mariamne e Mara" (literally, Mary known as the Master) and this is said to refer to Mary Magdalene. Again, the precise nature of the inscription is uncertain. It could also mean Martha, daughter of Mariamne; or Mariamne also known as Martha. Francis Bovon of Harvard Divinity School, who was interviewed in the documentary, subsequently commented in a letter to the Society of Biblical Literature in March 2007 (available on their

website) that he did not believe that Mariamne was the real name of Mary Magdalene, and that suggestions that Jesus and Mary were married and had a child "belong for me to science fiction".

3. A third ossuary bears the inscription "Yehuda bar Yeshua" said to mean Judah, son of Jesus. However, there is no evidence that Jesus ever did have a child (see Bovon's comment above).

4. The DNA tests only show that the bones found in the first two ossuaries were not of persons maternally related by blood. They do not (and could not) show that those persons were married. The documentary suggests that they were married, otherwise they would not be buried in the same tomb. However, they could have been paternally related, or Mariamne could have been married to one of the people in the other ossuaries (Yose, Matya, or one of the unnamed persons). There is no reason based on the evidence to conclude that the two were married.

5. No DNA tests were carried out on the bones found in the ossuary marked "Judah, son of Jesus" or on any of the other bones. This is surprising because of the suggestion that Judah was the son of Jesus and Mariamne, and a DNA test would have been the obvious way to establish this. Likewise, the other suggested blood relationships between the persons in the ossuaries could have been established (or disproved).

6. The names found – including Jesus, Joseph and Mary – were very common. We have already noted that Josephus refers to twenty people named Jesus. About one

in twenty Jewish men at the time were named Jesus, and one in three Jewish women were named Mary.

7. The statistical evidence is said to conclude that the odds are 600 to 1 in favour of this being the tomb of Jesus and his family. However, this calculation is based upon the other facts being correct – Jesus and Mary Magdalene being correctly identified and being married and having a son called Judah. If any of these facts is not established, then the statistical evidence is undermined. In particular, the alleged uniqueness of the "Mariamne e Mara" inscription hugely increased the odds.

8. The tenth ossuary went missing, and is alleged to be the "James Ossuary", the existence of which was announced in 2002. It bears the inscription "Ya'akov bar-Yosef akhui di Yeshua" (James, son of Joseph, brother of Jesus). However, the owner of the ossuary, Oded Golan was tried and acquitted on forgery charges, and as part of his defence he produced a photograph of the ossuary stamped March 1976, four years before the tomb was first uncovered.

9. As Jesus and his family were from Nazareth in Galilee, why would they have a family tomb in Jerusalem?

10. The conclusions in the documentary do not accord with the other available evidence, particularly that of Paul, James, Peter and the early church. See Appendix 3 for the importance of this point.

Appendix 3

Some Other (Bestselling) Theories

Books challenging the "traditional" understanding of Jesus and his resurrection are published on a relatively frequent basis. Some (such as *Jesus the Man* and *The Sign*) produce a genuinely novel theory. Others (such as *Holy Blood, Holy Grail*) reproduce a theory which has been suggested previously, albeit with additional evidence and novel elements. How is it possible for a lay person to evaluate the theories objectively? My suggestion is that any theory about Jesus' resurrection be approached in exactly the way set out in this book. In other words, it should be approached with an open mind, bearing in mind the burden and standard of proof. The theory can be analysed to see whether it deals with the various categories of evidence which we have considered, and if it does, how convincingly. A conclusion can then be reached as to whether the theory is reliable, or at least worthy of further research.

To illustrate this method, I have selected four very different theories and analysed them in this way. My criterion for selection was very basic – books that are currently available on the shelves of my local libraries. However, the same method can be used to consider any other theory, whether currently in print, out of print, or not yet written (for example that relating to the Talpiot Tomb – see Appendix 2).

1(a) *The Holy Blood and the Holy Grail*

Starting point

The Holy Blood and the Holy Grail (titled *Holy Blood, Holy Grail* in the United States) is a conspiracy theory on an epic scale. Starting with a mystery in the French village of Rennes-le-Château, it proceeds via the Cathar heresy and the Knights Templar to a secret society, the Priory of Sion, which is said to have existed for almost 1,000 years, and to be committed to the restoration of the Merovingian monarchy. The authors arrive at a hypothesis that there was a bloodline from Jesus to the Merovingians. They look for evidence to support that hypothesis, and claim to find it in the Gospels, in the context of the early church, and in early Christian writings. The hypothesis includes Jesus marrying Mary Magdalene, fathering one or more children, and surviving the crucifixion. The authors suggest that the New Testament portrait of Jesus conforms to the needs of vested interests, and that "everything else has been excised, creating a vacuum. In this vacuum speculation becomes both justified and necessary." It is worth noting here that juries are warned regularly not to speculate (which amounts to guesswork), although they are told that they may draw inferences from proven facts.

Paul

The Holy Blood and the Holy Grail (HBHG) barely mentions Paul, merely stating that he and others sought to perpetuate Jesus' message by adapting it primarily for a Romanized audience. The authors therefore do not even ask what could have happened to change Paul's life, and therefore do not suggest any answer.

James

The authors suggest that Jesus' followers were divided between his family, together with those who wanted to see Jesus as actual King of Israel, and the common people, who wanted to see his message of liberation fulfilled. When Jesus' mission "failed", his family sought to preserve his bloodline, while his other followers sought to perpetuate his message. This led to the family becoming "superfluous", and indeed an embarrassment because they could have "exploded the myth" that was constructed around Jesus. Therefore the family had to be "exterminated" by the church.

The authors fail to consider James' role in the early church, which is completely inconsistent with this hypothesis.

Peter

Presumably Peter is included among the followers of Jesus who were determined to "deify" Jesus, and for whom the resurrection "assumed critical importance" so as "to place Jesus on a par with other dying/rising gods". Again HBHG completely fails to deal with the change in Peter's life and what could have led to that.

It is also worth noting that there were many other "failed" messiahs shortly before, during, and after Jesus' lifetime, some of whom seem to have had a much larger popular following than Jesus, yet there was no attempt by their followers to "deify" them. HBHG fails to ask what marked Jesus out as different.

The early church

HBHG fails to deal in any coherent way with the early church. The suggestion that the resurrection was required so as to deify Jesus in order to perpetuate his message simply does not accord with the information available about the early church. This suggests that the church started with the fact of the resurrection, and gradually moved to the conclusion that he was divine (see

HBHG Chapter 20). The statement in the introduction that "the core of Christianity... resides in Jesus' teaching" does not accord with all the evidence about the teaching and practice of the early church, all of which places the resurrection at the core.

There is a comment in HBHG about Sundays, namely that Christians "held the Sabbath as sacred" until the time of Constantine, when this was transferred to Sunday. However, as Professor Chadwick points out on page 128 of *The Early Church* (a work which the authors of HBHG rely upon for other information), Christians began to observe Sunday in recollection of Jesus' death at a very early stage, and certainly before 1 Corinthians was written – some 250 years before Constantine! Also, the authors refer to the "tenacity" of heretics in the face of persecution, but fail to observe the same tenacity among "orthodox" early Christians, particularly those who claimed to have seen the risen Jesus.

Evidence outside the New Testament

Not surprisingly, the authors of HBHG consider the references to Jesus in Josephus to "conform to the Jesus of orthodoxy", and state that most modern scholars consider them to be "spurious interpolations". As we have seen, that is incorrect – most scholars accept that some of Josephus' references are authentic. HBHG also refers to the so-called "Slavonic Josephus" which suggests a very different picture of Jesus. This is a reference to Slavonic manuscripts discovered in the nineteenth century, which most modern scholars consider to be of highly dubious authenticity.

The Gospels

The authors of HBHG consider that the discrepancies between the Gospels mean they are of "highly questionable authority, and certainly not ... definitive". They also suggest that they were written for political reasons – to absolve the Romans of blame for Jesus' death. Further, they consider the Gospels to be an arbitrary selection of books and ask, "How can such a process of selection possibly be regarded as definitive?" The process to which they refer is that undertaken under Constantine, and the authors say that "the New Testament, as it exists today, is essentially a product of fourth-century editors and writers…with vested interests to protect". However, we have already seen in Appendix 1 that this is incorrect – the Gospels (and other New Testament books) were written in the first and second centuries, were recognized as authoritative by Christian leaders in those centuries, and were widely quoted by them. There undoubtedly were editorial changes made at different times, but the volume of manuscripts available, dating both before and after the fourth century, means that scholars can be very certain what the original text is likely to have said (with a few notable exceptions, such as the ending of Mark).

Other theories

The authors subscribe to the theory that Jesus survived the crucifixion as part of "a carefully contrived plan" and "a complex and ingenious stratagem/hoax". They suggest either that Jesus was given a soporific drug so as to simulate death, or that a substitute took his place. They say that it does not matter what then happened to Jesus.

This theory bears all the hallmarks of conspiracy theories that we identified in Chapter 17:

- They identify a number of conspirators: Jesus, Mary Magdalene, Jesus' family, and Joseph of Arimathea. In addition, they say that the connivance of Pilate or someone influential in the Roman administration was "highly probable".

- They use very selective parts of the Gospels to support the theory, while disregarding anything which runs counter to the theory. For example, they rely on John's account of Jesus being given wine to drink, and of Jesus' legs not being broken, but completely ignore the verses that follow, which speak of the piercing of his side.

- They attribute to the disciples astonishing stupidity. Their only attempts to explain the resurrection appearances are the possibility that an emissary of the plotters went to the tomb to reassure the unsuspecting disciples, and the alleged subsequent need to stress the resurrection so as to place Jesus on a par with other dying/reviving gods.

- They are based on no actual evidence at all, but on speculation. For example, in support of their hypothesis the authors refer to the second-century gnostic teacher Basilides, who taught that Simon of Cyrene died in Jesus' place. However, the relevant passage[54] reads as follows:

Wherefore he did not himself suffer death, but Simon, a certain man of Cyrene, being compelled, bore the cross in his stead; so that this latter being transfigured by him, that he might be thought to be Jesus, was crucified, through ignorance and error, while Jesus himself received the form of Simon, and, standing by, laughed at them. For since he was an incorporeal power, and the Nous [mind] of the unborn Father, he transfigured himself as he pleased, and thus ascended to him who had sent him, deriding them, inasmuch as he could not be laid hold of, and was invisible to all.

It is clear from this and other passages that Basilides taught that Jesus was not a man at all, but only appeared to be, and therefore he could not be physically crucified. Basilides' teaching was completely different from the hypothesis in HBHG, and does not support the hypothesis in any way.

Jesus

HBHG does not refer to Jesus' predictions of his resurrection. Apart from those made shortly before his crucifixion, they would be completely incompatible with the hypothesis in HBHG that Jesus was seeking to become the actual King of the Jews, only deciding on the crucifixion "hoax" when that plan failed.

Conclusion

The book has been widely criticized by historians as well as by Christian writers. The introduction to the 1996 edition declares that the scarcity of reliable information requires researchers to speculate within the framework of known historical information. However, the authors' speculation is notably always consistent with the hypothesis they are seeking to prove. To that end, they are extremely selective in their use of sources, using only those pieces of information which assist their arguments. One writer, not a Christian, has described the result as "a vast, elaborate and detailed alternative history, where each layer of speculation and wild hypothesis supported the next".[55] And in his judgment in Baigent & Leigh -v- Random House Group Ltd Mr Justice Peter Smith said (para 268), "Even as non-fiction it is doubtful whether the claimants have any genuine belief in the conjecture they present. That is why they call it historical conjecture."

While the hypothesis purports to explain the empty tomb and the missing body of Jesus, it does not begin to deal adequately with the resurrection appearances, the rise of the early church, or the dramatic change in the lives of Paul, James, and Peter.

1(b) *The Messianic Legacy*

Starting point

This is a sequel to HBHG, and indeed much material is repeated verbatim from HBHG. I therefore comment here only on the additional material.

The book starts from the promising statement that it is necessary to disregard any preconceptions, particularly those of tradition, and to consider the evidence dispassionately, as one would the life of Caesar or Alexander the Great. The authors go on to say that disbelief can be as much an act of faith as belief. However, they go on to suggest that probabilities and plausibilities should be balanced, and ask what is more likely to accord with humanity's experience – that Jesus married and tried to gain the throne of Israel, or that he rose from the grave. By asking this question, they move away from following the evidence to where it leads, and invite the answer already given in HBHG. They also appear only to be prepared to rely on certain types of evidence, for example "unbiased New Testament scholarship" (that is, based on their own view or bias, and so not "orthodox" or "conservative" scholarship).

Paul

The authors memorably say that "the midday sun at the time appears to have acted more dramatically than it subsequently does with mad dogs and Englishmen", and suggest that Paul's experience of the risen Jesus was actually sunstroke, an epileptic fit, or a mystical experience. I leave it to readers to decide for themselves whether this adequately deals with the wealth of evidence we have considered from Paul's letters and Acts (which the authors accept has a substantial historical element).

James

The authors note one of the Gospel references to James' opposition to Jesus and comment that this "was short lived ... within a short time of Jesus' death, he had taken his brother's place, had assumed the presiding role". They do not question why James' attitude changed, or consider Paul's reference to James experiencing the risen Jesus.

Peter

The authors suggest that Peter gravitated from James-and-Judaism to Paul-and-"Christianity" and was given new inspiration from an "elaborate rationalization" of what had happened to Jesus, which enabled him to continue preaching and to go boldly to martyrdom. Again, I leave it to readers to decide whether this adequately deals with the evidence about Peter which we have already considered.

The early church

A central premise of the book is that James and the "Nazarean Party" had no intention of creating a new religion, but were devout Jews working within the context of established Judaic tradition. It was the "heretic" Paul who created a new religion in which Jesus was divine and, therefore, had risen from the dead.

It is clear that there were divisions in the early church as they sought to work through issues such as the continuing effect of the Jewish ceremonial law, and we see this in Acts and many of Paul's letters. However, it is not clear how this analysis can explain the centrality of Jesus' resurrection in the preaching and practice of the early church from the outset, which again we see in Acts and Paul's letters. Moreover, the church appears to have derived their view of Jesus' divinity at least partly from his resurrection, rather than vice versa. The authors also acknowledge the very different nature of the kind of messiah expected by people at the time, without going on to ask why the church concluded that Jesus was the Messiah even though he was so totally different and unexpected.

Evidence outside the New Testament

The authors accept Tacitus' reference to Jesus as being "the one sure assertion about Jesus to issue from a non-biblical yet contemporary source".

Conclusion

The Messianic Legacy does purport to consider some of the evidence not considered in HBHG. However, in my view the explanations offered remain extremely weak and do not adequately explain the resurrection appearances, the rise of the early church, or the dramatic change in the lives of Paul, James, and Peter.

1(c) *The Jesus Papers*

This was written by one of the authors of HBHG, Michael Baigent, and is provocatively subtitled "Exposing the Greatest Cover-up in History". Much of the content repeats material in HBHG and *The Messianic Legacy*, but he presents two dramatic new pieces of evidence:

(1) A statement made to Baigent by a Revd Dr Bartlett, which he had been told fifty years earlier by his mentor, Canon Lilley, that Jesus was alive in the year AD 45 and that his survival was as a result of help from extreme zealots. Canon Lilley apparently based this statement on an original document which

he had translated forty or more years before he told Bartlett.

(2) Two papyrus texts shown to Baigent by an Israeli businessman and antiquities collector, which he was told were Aramaic letters from "bani meshiha" (the messiah of the children of Israel) to the Sanhedrin, defending himself against the charge of calling himself the son of God. As Baigent cannot read Aramaic, he was unable to verify this.

Neither of these would have any evidential value at all in a court. The first is multiple hearsay (what Baigent was told by Bartlett who was told by Lilley was contained in an unidentified document at least ninety years earlier, but without any detail as to the nature or actual content of the document), and the second is unattributed hearsay (what an unidentified person told Baigent about two documents). Neither is capable of independent verification.

Baigent is happy to rely on statements in the Gospels which support his theories, while rejecting those statements which do not. (Indeed, he even rejects Bartlett's reference to "extreme zealots" as being opinion rather than fact. His theory is that zealots demanded Jesus' death, so Bartlett's comment would not fit in with this theory.)

This approach enables Baigent to reach the remarkable conclusion that there is *no evidence* that Jesus died on the cross: particularly remarkable in the light of his acceptance of Tacitus' reference in *The Messianic Legacy*! He then asks where that leaves the resurrection, and answers that "these claims all disintegrate once the spin stops" and "all these assertions about Jesus came much later, the result of a glossy gift-wrapping of some historical events which were deliberately distorted in order to serve a strict theological agenda". It is obvious that he can only reach this conclusion by ignoring or disregarding the evidence of Matthew, Mark, Luke, John, Peter in Acts, Paul's letters, Josephus, Tacitus, the Talmud, and the early church fathers.

In reality, there is no evidence that Jesus survived the crucifixion.

2. *The Resurrection* by Geza Vermes

Starting point

Vermes was Professor Emeritus of Jewish studies at the University of Oxford. He had a fascinating personal background: born to Jewish parents who died in the holocaust, he became a Roman Catholic priest but subsequently left the church and returned to the Jewish faith. He accepted that Jesus was a real person who was crucified and buried. In attempting to discover what gave rise to the early church, he rejected what he called the "extreme" reactions of faith and disbelief, but set out as a detective to investigate what the Bible actually says.

Paul

Vermes suggests that Paul and other New Testament authors took for granted Jesus' resurrection (whatever that meant) and sought to derive doctrines from it. In Paul's case, he suggests that Paul was not aware of, or chose not to mention, the empty tomb and the disappearance of Jesus' body, and that he turned the resurrection into the centrepiece of his theology without the need to rely on such historical details. He also suggests that Paul's comments in 1 Corinthians 15 may be influenced by political considerations – he was seeking to assert equality with Peter and James. He does not consider at all what could have produced such a radical change in Paul's life.

James and Peter

Likewise, Vermes does not consider what could have produced such a radical change in the lives of James and Peter, even though he does accept as authentic the "dishonourable conduct" of the disciples in abandoning Jesus to his death.

The early church

Vermes concludes that "the conviction of the spiritual presence of the living Jesus accounts for the resurgence of the Jesus movement", and describes this as "resurrection in the hearts of men" and "a helping hand" in their task of preaching the gospel. However, he does not consider why the resurrection so quickly became the centrepiece of the Christian faith, other than by apparently attributing this to Paul.

Evidence outside the New Testament

Vermes accepts that the first part of the Testimonium Flavianum may be authentic, and may show a belief in spiritual resurrection. He rejects the remainder (from "on the third day") as being a Christian interpolation.

The Gospels

Vermes places considerable weight upon the discrepancies between the four Gospel accounts. He treats Mark as having originally ended at 16:8, and so uses the longer and shorter endings as different sources when considering discrepancies. He does not consider whether Mark intended to finish at 16:8, and he does not consider at all any of the factors suggesting that the accounts may be authentic.

Other theories

Vermes accepts that there was an early tradition of the empty tomb, which is not invented because it is far from a "uniform and foolproof account attributed to patently reliable witnesses", as would be the case if it had been invented. He goes on to consider the other theories that may explain this:

1. The body was moved – not likely as the mover could have explained this.

2. The body was stolen by the disciples – there is no doubt that this is later Jewish gossip.

3. The disciples went to the wrong tomb – not likely, as they could have checked with Joseph of Arimathea.

4. Jesus did not die, but disappeared – not very likely, and what happened to him?

5. Jesus did not die, but became a migrant – "in the absence of real ancient evidence these recent modern musings need not detain us".

6. Spiritual resurrection – the viewers had visions which they believed were real. However, there would then be no need for an empty tomb.

Jesus

Vermes notes the surprising lack of teaching by Jesus about resurrection, but considers Jesus' predictions about his resurrection to be inauthentic because the disciples would not have been surprised by the resurrection had Jesus so clearly predicted it.

Conclusion

Vermes accepts that none of the other theories stands up to stringent scrutiny, which leaves the empty tomb as a conundrum. His conclusion that the disciples "felt increasingly sure that … Jesus was with them" does not resolve that conundrum. Nor, in my view, does it begin to explain the transformation in the lives of Paul and James.

3. *The Sign* by Thomas de Wesselow

Starting Point

De Wesselow is an art historian "experienced at tackling 'unsolvable' problems", and this book falls into two distinct divisions. In the first, de Wesselow undertakes an extensive review of all the evidence relating to the Turin Shroud. In the second, he considers the resurrection in the light of his conclusions in relation to the shroud.

In summary, his conclusions are as follows:

1. Something extraordinary must have happened in the wake of Jesus' death to give rise to the church. "The Resurrection-shaped hole in history cannot simply be dismissed as a mirage."

2. "When faced with a mysterious phenomenon, it is generally wise to presume that it has a natural cause."

3. Despite the negative carbon-dating test, the shroud is the genuine burial shroud of Jesus.

4. The images on the shroud were not formed supernaturally, but by some chemical reaction between Jesus' corpse and the fibres of the shroud.

5. The shroud is not evidence of a physical resurrection, but was interpreted as a kind of resurrection.

6. Therefore Christianity is based on a colossal mistake – the mistaking of a chemical reaction for resurrection.

The first point is precisely that made in Chapter 6 of this book, but the second operates to rule out possible answers to the first without considering the evidence (see Chapter 3 of this book).

No body

De Wesselow suggests that the fate of Jesus' body was irrelevant because the shroud revealed his new, resurrection body. Therefore his body remained in the tomb and would have been reburied after a year. "The Jerusalem church presumably honoured the site of Jesus' mortal remains, but once his immediate family died, few would have given much thought to Jesus' bones ... precise knowledge of the place may have been lost during the Jewish war." He considers the idea of the empty tomb to be a late first-century invention.

This stretches belief. It seems extremely unlikely, given the veneration by the Jews of the tombs of their leaders, that the location of Jesus' tomb could simply have been forgotten. If the tomb was "honoured", it is surprising that it is not mentioned in *any* early Christian literature. To the contrary, Acts 2:29–92 expressly states that Jesus' body was not subject to decay in a tomb.

Paul

De Wesselow speculates that Paul travelled to Damascus to hunt down the shroud, and that he then had an overwhelming spiritual experience when confronted with the shroud, which he interpreted as Jesus' resurrection. De Wesselow places huge weight on 1 Corinthians 15 as being a very early creed (verses 3–7) and a clear statement that the resurrection will not involve "flesh and blood" (verses 35–54). However, although he makes numerous references to *The Resurrection of the Son of God* by N. T. Wright, he does not deal with Wright's conclusion, on page 372 after 160 pages of detailed analysis, that Paul "believed, and articulated in considerable detail, that the resurrection would not only be bodily... but that it would also involve *transformation*".

Furthermore, as with all the other appearances (which de Wesselow attributes to viewings of the shroud), one has to ask whether this would actually have been sufficient to produce the fundamental change in Paul's life reflected in his letters and Acts.

We might also ask why not one Christian writer in the first century makes any explicit reference to the shroud, apart from the account in the Gospel of John which appears to leave it in the tomb as surplus to requirements.

James

De Wesselow interprets the appearance to James, referred to in 1 Corinthians 15, as a ritualistic showing of the shroud by Peter and the rest of the disciples. However, can this sensibly be described (by Paul) as an "appearance"?

Peter

De Wesselow suggests that when Peter first discovered the shroud in the tomb, he did not immediately believe. He suggests that the Gospels were written to pursue a pro-Magdalene/ matriarchal agenda, and therefore do not list an appearance to Peter. Some very much later sources (from the ninth and thirteenth centuries, though these may in part date back to the fourth or fifth) are relied on to show that Peter did then remove the shroud from the tomb and used to wear it (folded) on his head to achieve miraculous healings. (De Wesselow, following Ian Wilson, identifies the "Mandylion", a relic known to exist long before the earliest record of the shroud, as being the shroud folded into eight so as only to display the face of Jesus.) An obvious question is why none of this is mentioned in any of the biblical or non-canonical early Christian documents?

The early church

De Wesselow helpfully identifies five aspects of the "puzzle" of Christianity which are difficult to understand:

1. It was inspired by a crucifixion – "the most extraordinary reaction to an execution!"

2. Jesus was hailed as Messiah – "what could possibly have prompted the first Nazareans to hijack the nationalistic idea of the Messiah and apply it to the pitiable figure of Jesus?"

3. The obsession with resurrection, particularly the abandonment of the link seen in Ezekiel between resurrection and the resurgence of Israel.

4. Adoption of Sunday as a day of worship at a very early date.

5. Why did it not disappear? How did it achieve the necessary critical mass?

He contends that the finding of the shroud and subsequent scriptural reflection upon it provides an explanation. Again, the obvious question is why *no* documents which emerged from the early church mention the shroud. De Wesselow's explanation is, essentially, that by the time the Gospels were written, the church had forgotten about the shroud. This seems to me to be the weakest point in the book. Even assuming a very late date for the Gospels, it seems inconceivable that the shroud would not have been mentioned unambiguously in the much earlier documents, like Paul's letters.

Evidence outside the New Testament

De Wesselow accepts the evidence of Tacitus, Seutonius, Pliny, and Josephus (though not the Testimonium Flavium), and sees them as consistent with his conclusions.

The Gospels

De Wesselow considers the Gospels to have been written at the end of the first century by second- or third-generation Christians, and to be a mixture of fact and fiction. He treats some parts as entirely fictional (for example, the road to Emmaus), some as largely factual (the appearances to the women, although what is recorded as angels and Jesus is actually the shroud), and some as a mixture (the appearance to the Twelve, which was actually Peter showing them the shroud; the recorded words of Jesus are fictional). This enables him to use parts of the Gospel which support his thesis while ignoring parts which do not, and often that appears to be the only criterion he adopts in distinguishing fact from fiction!

Other theories

Interestingly, de Wesselow considers that over the last 150 years the failure to solve the "Resurrection problem" with a non-miraculous explanation has become chronic, and that there are major difficulties with the "weird and wonderful" solutions which have been suggested. "The secret of the Resurrection has turned out to be as elusive as the Snark." I agree wholeheartedly with this, but would include his solution, with its major difficulties, as part of the "weird and wonderful".

Conclusion

De Wesselow's analysis of the evidence as to the authenticity of the Turin shroud is carried out in a very thorough manner, and his conclusions about this are very thought-provoking. However, his analysis of the evidence as to the resurrection is of a wholly different nature. It is highly selective, and does not satisfactorily explain much of the evidence. Particularly extraordinary is the idea that the early church rapidly forgot about the shroud to the extent that it was not mentioned at all in their documents despite being the sole foundation of their belief in the resurrection!

4. *Jesus the Man* by Barbara Thiering

Starting Point

Thiering describes how she became deeply involved in the church, but then became restless about its doctrines and eventually came to terms with Christianity "only by seeing it as a symbolic language, pointing to something that could not be expressed in words". She devotes considerable time to studying the Dead Sea Scrolls, and concludes that they did in fact refer to Jesus. She explains the "*pesher*" technique used in the scrolls, where Old Testament texts are given a *pesher* (essentially a coded) meaning for the time of the writer. So, for example, references to Babylon have a *pesher* meaning of Rome. She goes on to suggest that the Gospel writers set out to write in *pesher* style, so that the true story of Jesus is concealed within the text. So, for example, the story of Jesus turning water into wine represents Jesus allowing lower-grade members of the community to receive communion. In relation to the resurrection, the true meaning of the texts is that Jesus survived the crucifixion and stayed with his followers for many years.

Paul

Thiering states that the true meaning of the account in Acts of Paul seeing Jesus is that Jesus was acting as priest at a service in Qumran. As was the tradition, he was on the roof, and when the "half-roof" was removed, the sun shone in Paul's eyes and Jesus spoke to him. As Paul then listened to the sermon, "his strenuous objections to all that Jesus stood for began to dissolve".

I cannot begin to see how this explains Paul's extensive references to the resurrection in his letters. This is ingenious theorizing at a new level.

James

James is presented by Thiering as a complex character, at times supporting Jesus and at times behaving treacherously toward him. Thiering identifies him as Cleopas in the encounter on the road to Emmaus in Luke 24 – he did not "recognize" Jesus in the sense of not recognizing him as the legitimate heir. However, as Jesus blessed the bread "as a king", James changed his mind. He subsequently remained with the Jewish Christians, but did not teach the resurrection.

This identification of James as Cleopas is entirely unconvincing. Why would Luke call him Cleopas here when he calls him James throughout Acts? And the interpretation of the encounter with Jesus does not accord at all with the actual text of Luke's description.

Peter

Thiering deals only with a few of the incidents involving Peter. She does not deal specifically with Jesus' appearance to him, but states that the true meaning of Jesus' appearances to his ministers was that he attended the set services on the sabbath over the next few days – so they were amazed "not at a resurrection, but at the strength and dedication which had enabled him to recover". Peter's subsequent preaching that Jesus had been "raised up" actually meant that he had been promoted to a higher status at Qumran. This is, of course, completely at odds with Luke's account of Peter's preaching in Acts, and does not explain at all Paul's reference to Jesus appearing to Peter.

The early church and the Gospels

Thiering states that Jesus remained with his followers for many years after the crucifixion, ultimately travelling to Rome with Paul. Further, he was behind the writing of the Gospels, which she therefore gives a very early date (from John in AD 37 to Acts in AD 63): "Although the style of each gospel is different… it is difficult to avoid the impression … that a single mind lies behind them." No other scholar, however theologically conservative, has suggested such early dates for all the Gospels. It is also extraordinary, if Thiering is correct, that (1) no early Christian literature refers to the fact that Jesus not only survived the crucifixion but went on to be active in the church, and (2) the church at a very early stage forgot that the Gospels were written as *pesher*, and interpreted them literally.

Evidence outside the New Testament

The only evidence referred to by Thiering is the comment by Tacitus, which appears at the very end of the body of her book (before the very extensive appendices). She quotes this without comment or question, despite Tacitus' reference to Jesus undergoing "the death penalty", which seems flatly to contradict her view that Jesus did not die.

Other theories

Thiering states that Jesus took snake poison on the cross, and lost consciousness. Simon Magus and Judas were crucified with him. Their legs were broken, but Jesus' were not as he was believed to be dead. Instead, his side was pierced. All three were placed in two adjacent tombs with a stone across the entrance, and Simon and Judas were left to die. Medicines were left near to Jesus, and sympathizers entered the tomb and carried Simon to Jesus to administer them. The three of them then escaped with the help of the guards. All of this took place at Qumran, not Jerusalem.

Even accepting the *pesher* theory, it is difficult to know where to start with this explanation. Is it possible that Jesus, having been whipped, crucified, poisoned, and stabbed, would be able to escape from a tomb with the assistance of a man who had been crucified and had both his legs broken? Why do Thiering's explanations of the Gospel accounts contain a mixture of literal and *pesher* meanings? It is difficult to avoid the conclusion that Thiering uses words in the same way as Humpty Dumpty in *Alice Through the Looking Glass* – when she uses a word, it means just what she chooses it to mean.

Conclusion

Thiering's work is so detailed and specific in its conclusions that a lay reader would hesitate before challenging it. However, experts have not hesitated to do so. Vermes states that the book "has made no impact on learned opinion" and comments that not one of the 813 Qumran documents verifies her "recipe of composition". He considers that the Gospels are her only "proof" that they were written in *pesher* style – in other words, her theory about this is wholly circular. (Vermes' reply to Thiering's letter commenting on his review of the book can be found on the *New York Review of Books* website.) Dr C. B. Forbes describes the work as "an eccentric theory based on weak historical evidence, sloppy logic, and wild guesswork" and states that her theory about the resurrection is "such an extraordinary fantasy that it almost defies comment".[56]

Appendix 4

Easter Enigma

This appendix is a summary of John Wenham's book *Easter Enigma*, which is subtitled "Do the Resurrection Stories Contradict One Another?" The author does an impressive job of dealing with all the apparent problems, although it has to be conceded that Christian readers are more likely to be satisfied with some of his solutions than sceptical readers. If you wish to review the argument in detail you would be well advised to read the book and not just the summary.

John Wenham comments that the Gospel resurrection accounts "differ from each other to an astonishing degree. So much so that distinguished scholars one after another have said categorically that the five accounts [including 1 Corinthians 15] are irreconcilable" (page 9). But he goes on to conclude that "it now seems to me that these resurrection stories exhibit in a remarkable way the well-known characteristics of accurate and independent reporting, for superficially they show great disharmony, but on close examination the details gradually fall into place" (page 11).

Wenham considers the identity of the women who witnessed the crucifixion, and concludes that:

- Mary Magdalene is the same person as Mary of Bethany.

- Salome (in Mark) is Jesus' mother's sister (in John), the mother of James and John, sons of Zebedee (in Matthew).

- Mary, the mother of James and Joses/Joseph (in Matthew and Mark) is the wife of Clopas in John (referred to as Cleopas and Alphaeus in Matthew, Mark, Luke, and Acts).

Wenham then identifies the likely Gospel sources as:

- Matthew – the Galilean women.

- Mark – Peter and Mary Magdalene.

- Luke – Joanna and Cleopas.

- John – John himself and Mary Magdalene.

He goes on to locate the characters as follows:

- At John's house – Peter, Mary Magdalene, Mary wife of Clopas, Jesus' mother, Salome, Zebedee and Clopas.

- At Bethany – the other disciples.

- At the Hasmonean Palace – Joanna and Susanna.

- On the Sabbath Eve, Mary Magdalene, Clopas, and Mary travel from John's house to Bethany.

The Gospel accounts are then explained/reconciled in the following sequence:

1. Mary Magdalene and Mary went to the tomb from Bethany (Matthew 28:1–15), via John's house, collecting Salome from there.

2. Mary Magdalene rushed from the tomb to tell Peter and John (John 20:1).

3. Joanna and Susanna arrived at the tomb.

4. The women went into the tomb (Matthew 28:5–7; Mark 16:5–7; Luke 24:3–8). The young man of Mark was an angel.

5. The women went to tell the disciples and no one else (Matthew 28:8; Mark 16:8; Luke 24: 9–11).

6. Peter and John ran to the tomb (John 20; Luke 24:12) and returned home.

7. Mary Magdalene went to the tomb (John 20:11–18).

8. Mary wife of Clopas and Salome set off to Bethany to tell the disciples, and Jesus met them (the disciples meaning the brethren, not just the apostles) (Matthew 28:8–10).

9. Clopas and another disciple go to Emmaus (Mark 16:12; Luke 24:13–31).

10. They later returned and told the others (Luke 24:32–35; Mark 16:11).

11. Jesus appeared to the disciples (Luke 24:36–43; John 20:19–23; Paul's reference to Jesus appearing to "the Twelve" [1 Corinthians 15:5]).

12. Jesus appeared again to the disciples, this time including Thomas (John 20:24–29), they having stayed in Jerusalem for six days of Unleavened Bread over the Passover.

13. The Twelve returned to Galilee and met Jesus again there (John 21).

14. The great commission was given (Matthew 28:16–20 and Paul's reference to Jesus appearing to "more than 500").

15. Jesus appeared to James (Paul's reference).

16. Jesus' final appearance (Mark 16:15–20 and Paul's reference).

Appendix 5

The Ending of Mark

As discussed briefly in Chapter 14, there are various views held by scholars about the original ending of Mark's Gospel. A number of writers not only consider the original to have ended at 16:8, but also consider that to reflect the earliest tradition, which the other Gospel writers amplified by adding stories of resurrection appearances. In other words, the earliest tradition was of an empty tomb only, and the resurrection appearances were added at a later date.

Although I am not a biblical or literary scholar, it seems to me that there are a number of reasons which very strongly suggest that 16:8 was not the original ending. Some of these are dealt with much more fully in *The Resurrection of the Son of God* by N. T. Wright at pages 617–624, and these are marked below with an asterisk.

1. If 16:8 was the original ending, the Gospel did not so much end as come to a grinding halt. It is totally unsatisfactory from a literary point of view. A more modern equivalent would be Hercule Poirot gathering the cast together in the drawing room and saying, "After detailed investigation, I have ascertained that you all had a motive for this apparently baffling murder. Using my little grey cells I have worked out who the murderer is. But I'm not going to tell you." And then leaving. The preceding verses simply demand a conclusion.

2. In particular, verse 7 ("But go, tell his disciples and Peter, 'He is going ahead of you into Galilee. There you will see him, just as he told you.'") calls for resolution. Did the disciples go to Galilee or not? If they did, did they see Jesus? If they didn't, what did they do between Good Friday and Pentecost?

3. Such an ending could hardly be categorized as "good news" in 1:1. A brief life followed by an unjust death and unfulfilled predictions of resurrection would not be most people's idea of good news!

4.* We have seen in Chapter 18 that Jesus predicted his betrayal, suffering, death, and resurrection (Mark 8:31; 9:31; 10:32). It would be very odd if Mark intended to deal in detail with the betrayal, suffering, and death but to ignore completely the resurrection.

5.* The structure of the Gospel suggests a fuller ending. It falls into two parts. The first, chapters 1–8, builds up to the recognition of Jesus' messiahship, and concludes with a remarkable event – the transfiguration. The second part, chapters 9–15, builds up to Jesus' death and resurrection, and calls for the remarkable event of the resurrection.

Bibliography

Anchor Bible Dictionary, 1992, David Noel Freedman ed., Bantam Doubleday Dell.

Anderson, J. N. D., 1969, *Christianity, the Witness of History,* Tyndale Press.

-- 1950, *The Evidence for the Resurrection,* Inter-Varsity Fellowship.

Armstrong, Karen, 1993, 1999, *A History of God,* Random House.

Baigent, Michael, 2006, *The Jesus Papers,* Harper Element.

Baigent, Michael; Leigh, Richard; Lincoln, Henry; 1986, 1996, *The Holy Blood and the Holy Grail,* Arrow.

-- 1986, 1996, *The Messianic Legacy,* Jonathan Cape.

Barclay, William, 1954, 1975, *The Letters to the Corinthians*, Saint Andrew Press.

Barnett, Paul, 1986, *Is the New Testament History?,* Hodder & Stoughton.

Bingham, Tom, 2000, *The Business of Judging,* Oxford University Press.

Black's Medical Dictionary, Harvey Marcovitch ed., 42nd edition, 2009, A & C Black.

British Medical Association's Illustrated Medical Dictionary, 2007, Dorling Kindersley.

Brown, Dan, 2003, *The Da Vinci Code,* Anchor Books.

Bruce, F. F., 1943, 1960, *The New Testament Documents – Are They Reliable?,* Inter-Varsity Press.

-- 1955, 1984, *The Books and the Parchments,* Revell.

Carr, E. H., 1961, *What Is History?*, Cambridge University Press.

Chadwick, Henry, 1967, 1993, *The Early Church,* The Penguin History of the Church 1, Penguin.

Bibliography

Copi, Irving; Cohen, Carl; McMahon, Kenneth; 1953, 2010, *Introduction to Logic,* Pearson.

Dawkins, Richard, 2006, *The God Delusion,* Bantam Press.

De Wesselow, Thomas, 2012, *The Sign,* Penguin.

Edwards, William; Gabel, Wesley; Hosmer, Floyd; 1986, "On the Physical Death of Jesus Christ", *Journal of the American Medical Association,* Vol. 255, No.11.

Elton, G. R., 1969, *The Practice of History,* Fontana.

Evans, C. F., 1965, *The New Testament Gospels,* BBC.

Feldman, Louis, 1984, *Josephus and Modern Scholarship 1937–1980,* Walter de Gruyter.

Festinger, Leon, and others, 1956, 2008, *When Prophecy Fails: A Social and Psychological Study of a Modern Group that Predicted the Destruction of the World,* University of Minnesota Press.

Foster, Charles, 2006, *The Jesus Inquest,* Monarch.

Greenleaf, Simon, 1847, *An Examination of the Testimony of the Four Evangelists by the Rules of Evidence Administered in Courts of Justice,* A Maxwell & Son.

Habermas, Gary and Licona, Michael, 2004, *The Case for the Resurrection of Jesus,* Kregel.

Hill, C. E., 2010, *Who Chose the Gospels?* Probing the Great Gospel Conspiracy, Oxford University Press.

Kenyon, Sir Frederic, 1940, *The Bible and Archaeology,* Harrap.

Lake, Kirsopp, 1907, *The Historical Evidence for the Resurrection of Jesus Christ,* Williams & Norgate.

Lewis, C. S., 2000, *Essay Collection and Other Short Pieces,* HarperCollins.

-- 1975, *Fern Seeds and Elephants,* Collins.

Martin, Ralph, 1975, *The Four Gospels,* New Testament Foundations 1, Paternoster.

Mason, Steve, 2003, *Josephus and the New Testament,* Baker.

McDowell, Josh, 1981, 1998, *Evidence that Demands a Verdict,* Paternoster.

-- and Bill Wilson, 2011, *Evidence for the Historical Jesus,* Harvest House.

Metzger, Bruce, and Ehrman, Bart, 1964, 2005, 4th ed., *The Text of the New Testament: Its Transmission, Corruption and Restoration*, Oxford University Press.

Montgomery, John Warwick, 1986, *History and Christianity*, Bethany House.

Morison, Frank, 1930, 2006, *Who Moved the Stone?*, Authentic.

Moule, C. F. D., 1967, *The Phenomenon of the New Testament*, SCM Press.

Murray, Stuart, 2004, *Post-Christendom,* Paternoster.

Oxford Companion to the Bible, 1993, 2004, Bruce Metzger and Michael Coogan ed., Oxford University Press.

Phipson on Evidence, 17th edition, 2012, Hodge Malek ed., Sweet & Maxwell.

Sanderson, Colin J., 2007, *Understanding Genes and GMOs*, World Scientific Publishing Co.

Sherwin-White, A. N., 1963, *Roman Society and Roman Law in the New Testament: The Sarum Lectures 1960–1961*, Oxford University Press.

Spufford, Francis, 2012, *Unapologetic,* Faber & Faber.

Strobel, Lee, 1998, *The Case for Christ,* Zondervan.

Thiede, Carsten Peter, 2005, *The Emmaus Mystery,* Continuum.

Thiering, Barabara, 1992, *Jesus the Man,* Doubleday.

Vermes, Geza, 2008, *The Resurrection*, Penguin.

Wenham, John, 1984, *Easter Enigma,* Paternoster.

Wright, N. T., 1996, *Jesus and the Victory of God,* SPCK.

–– 2002, *Matthew for Everyone,* SPCK.

–– 2000, *The Challenge of Jesus,* SPCK.

–– 1992, *The New Testament People of God,* SPCK.

–– 2003, *The Resurrection of the Son of God,* SPCK.

–– 1992, *Who Was Jesus?*, SPCK.

Young, John, 1986, 2006, *The Case Against Christ,* Hodder & Stoughton.

Notes

1. *Christianity* magazine, February 2013, page 74.

2. *Christianity* magazine, February 2013, page 23.

3. In the version published by the English Language Liturgical Consultation.

4. See 3.47 for the virgin birth, 5.110 for miracles, 4.171 for denial of Jesus' divinity and 4.156–158 for denial of death and resurrection. All references are to surahs (chapters) and ayahs (verses) of the Qur'an.

5. Baigent & Leigh -v- Random House Group Ltd [2006] EWHC 719(Ch), para 46. The judgment was upheld by the Court of Appeal, [2007] EWCA Civ 247. Smith J. also said in his judgment, referring to *The Da Vinci Code*, "Of course merely because an author of fiction describes matters as being factually correct does not mean that they are factually correct. It is a way of blending fact and fiction together to create that well known model 'faction'. The lure of apparent genuineness makes the books and the films more receptive to the readers/audiences. The danger of course is that the faction is all that large parts of the audience read and they accept it as truth" (para 81).

6. A slightly less definitive statement was used in a bus advertising campaign which started in 2009 – "There's probably no God. Now stop worrying and enjoy your life." The Advertising Standards Authority ruled that this was an expression of opinion and was not capable of substantiation.

7. Sir Richard Scott VC in Victor Chandler International Ltd -v- Customs & Excise Commissioners [2000] 1 WLR 1296, at page 1302.

8. *Phipson on Evidence*, 2012, para 1–13.

9. Cresswell J. in National Justice Compania Naviera SA -v- Prudential Assurance Co Ltd (The "Ikarian Reefer") [1993] 2 Lloyd's Rep 68, at pages 81–82.

10. *Phipson*, para 1–14.

11. *Phipson*, para 1–13.

12. The information in this table is taken from various sources, including John Young, *The Case Against Christ* and Paul H. Barrett, *Is the New Testament History?*

13. As at 2003 this figure included all Greek manuscripts and fragments. Only about sixty contain the entire New Testament. Most of the others contain either the Gospels or the Epistles. In addition, there are thousands of other manuscripts in other languages. See Chapter 2 of Metzger and Ehrman 1964, 2005, for full details.

14. *The Art of the Soluble*, Oxford University Press 1967, quoted in Sanderson 2007, page 1.

15. "The Judge as Juror: The Judicial Determination of Factual Issues" in Bingham 2000.

16. See N. T. Wright, 2003, Chapters 3 and 4, for a very full survey of the development of belief in resurrection in the Old Testament and post-biblical literature.

17. Roger Gray, barrister of 5 Pump Court Chambers, in *Christian Lawyer* magazine, Autumn 2004.

18. See also, for example, Romans 3:24–25; 5:6–10; 6:3–10.

19. Roger Gray, barrister of 5 Pump Court Chambers, in *Christian Lawyer* magazine, Autumn 2004.

20. Acts 12:2 makes it clear that this is not a reference to James the brother of John, who had already been killed.

21. See also Matthew 26:33–35. The accounts in Luke 22:31–34 and John 13:37–38 are slightly different, but still predict Peter's denial.

22. From the judgment of the Court of Appeal in R -v- Onufrejczyk, which upheld a conviction for murder despite the fact that the body of the victim had not been found.

23. BBC News website, 4 February 2013.

24. The website's "historical sources" include the *Life of St Issa* scroll. Allegedly seen by Russian aristocrat Nicolas Notovitch in a monastery in 1887, the scroll allegedly records Jesus' lost years in India. The existence of the scroll is strongly disputed, but in any event it records that Jesus returned to, and was put to death in, Jerusalem.

25. Sam Miller, at http:// news.bbc.co.uk/ 1/ hi/ programmes/ from_our_ own_correspondent/ 8587838.stm

26. See for example Peter's sermons in Acts 2 and 3; his defence before the Sanhedrin in Acts 4; his testimony to Cornelius in Acts 10. See also the references to other early Christian writers in Chapter 12.

27. See Charles Foster (2006), pages 198–200 for details of the traditions. Ignatius in his letter to Smyrna and Polycarp in his letter to the Philippians also mention the suffering of the apostles.

28. The full text can be found at www.archbishopofcanterbury.org/articles

29. Matthew, Mark, Luke, John, Paul, James, Peter, Jude, and the writer of Hebrews.

30. Clement of Rome, 2 Clement, Ignatius, Polycarp, The Martyrdom of Polycarp, Didache, Barnabas, the Shepherd of Hermas, Papias, Justin Martyr, Aristides, Athenagoras, Theophilus of Antioch, Quadratus, Aristo of Pella, Melito of Sardis, Diognetus, Gospel of Peter, Apocalypse of Peter, Epistula Apostolorum.

31. Gospel of Thomas, Gospel of Truth, Apocrypha of John, Treatise on Resurrection.

32. Josephus, Tacitus, Pliny, Phlegon, Lucian, Celsus, Mara Bar-Serapion, Seutonius, Thallus.

33. There is also a disputed passage at 25.4 of the *Life of Claudius* which refers to "Chrestus". It is not clear that this is a reference to Jesus, but from a historical perspective it is interesting that the passage accords with what Luke says in Acts 18:2.

34. For more on this view, see Anderson 1969, page 19.

35. For a full survey, see McDowell and Wilson 2011.

36. For example, *First Apology*, Chapter 12. Fragments exist of a work "on the resurrection", which as the name suggests makes extensive reference to the resurrection; but it is not accepted by all scholars that he was the author.

37. For example, the "John Rylands fragment", now to be found in the John Rylands library in Manchester, wholly disproved Baur's theory that John's Gospel was written as late as AD 160–180.

38. See also John 21:25, with obvious hyperbole!

39. For a detailed critique see, for example, W. L. Craig, "Rediscovering the historical Jesus" on his www.reasonablefaith.org website.

40. See Metzger and Ehrman 1964, 2005 page 126; see also McDowell, 1981, 1998, pages 50–52, for the detail.

41. Charles Foster, 2006, page 145. His Christian opponent responds on page 160.

42. Dating from the fourth century, this includes the only known complete copy of the Greek New Testament in majuscule script – see Metzger and Ehrman 1964, 2005, pages 62–66.

43. These comprise fragments of the four Gospels, Acts, and most of the other New Testament books, dating from the early third century – see Metzger & Ehrman, 1964, 2005, pages 54–55.

44. *The Times*, 6 August 2012, in a review by Salley Vickers of Rowan Williams', *The Lion's World*.

45. From "What Are We to Make of Jesus Christ?" in Lewis 2000, page 40.

46. Para 29, upon which he elaborates in paras 30–48.

47. Sir Arthur Conan Doyle, *The Sign of the Four*, in *Lippincott's* magazine 1890.

48. Edwards, Gabel, and Hosmer, "On the Physical Death of Jesus Christ" in the *Journal of the American Medical Association* 1986, Vol. 255, No. 11, page 1455.

49. Sir Arthur Conan Doyle, *A Scandal in Bohemia*, 1892, George Newnes.

50. Francis Nagaraya, Myers F. W. H. et al. (1894), "Report on the Census of Hallucinations", *Proceedings of the Society for Psychical Research* 34:25–394; West D. J. (1948), "A Mass Observation Questionnaire on Hallucinations", *Journal of the Society for Psychical Research*, 34, 187–96; Ohayon M. M. (Dec. 2000), "Prevalence of Hallucinations and Their Pathological Associations in the General Population", *Psychiatry Res* 97 (2–3): 153–64.

51. Susanna Clarke, 2004, *Jonathan Strange and Mr Norrell: A Novel*, Bloomsbury, page 773.

52. For a succinct summary see N. T. Wright, 2003, pages 731–36.

53. The story was originally told by the preacher John Hutton, and is quoted in William Barclay, 1954, 1975, page 25.

54. None of Basilides' writings survive. The information available about Basilides is found in *Against Heresies*, Book 1, Chapter 24, and the quotation is from Section 4.

55. Tim O'Neill, on his website "History versus the Da Vinci Code", commenting on Chapter 23. Mr O'Neill describes himself as an atheist with an interest in the study of medieval history, medieval literature, and ancient history, with a particular interest in the origins of Christianity, the formation of the Bible, and the history of the early church.

56. Available online at http://web.archive.org/web/20110716080336/http://www.anchist.mq.edu.au/251/Thierful.htm